to Wilma White
Best Wishes

What Makes
a Marriage Work?

Printed in Canada.

For information address:
Durban House Publishing Company, Inc.
7502 Greenville Avenue, Suite 500, Dallas, Texas 75231

Library of Congress Cataloging-in-Publication Data
Mahr, Malcolm D., 1928

What Makes a Marriage Work? / Malcolm D. Mahr

Library of Congress Catalog Number: 2003115814

p. cm.

ISBN 1-930754-47-7

First Edition

10 9 8 7 6 5 4 3 2 1

Visit our Web site at
http://www.durbanhouse.com

What Makes a Marriage Work?

*If you want the rainbow,
you gotta put up with the rain*

BY

MALCOLM D. MAHR

Dedication

This book is dedicated with deepest love and affection to Fran, my beloved wife of 50 years.

Fran, in 1951, after we were married for only ten days, my Army Reserve was activated, and I ended up in Korea. You, Fran, were very devoted.

In 1993 when my business went into bankruptcy, and I was out of a job, you stood by me, Fran darling.

And in 1994 when they couldn't find a urologist—in all of Johns Hopkins Hospital—to put in a catheter, and I had to endure a painful urinary blockage for hours and hours, you never left my bedside.

To tell you the truth, Fran, I'm beginning to think you're BAD LUCK!

Contents

Thank You

Cartoons What soap is to the body, cartoons are to the soul. People like to laugh, but there's also a serious side to humor. A good cartoon has three characteristics: a comical truth, a few words, and a fine image.

My thanks to Jennifer Konig and Merrideth Miller of The Cartoon Bank Division of *The New Yorker Magazine,* for helping me select from their archives of thousands of cartoons.

Proverbs Robert Peter Tristram Coffin said, "Proverbs are not merely decorations on life, they have life itself in them. They are the beginnings of all literature, the first metaphors and similes, the first comedies and tragedies, they are the first poetry we have."

Ger de Ley's *International Dictionary of Proverbs* is an excellent source of proverbs from around the world, and I recommend it for further reading.

Foreword

The way I see it, if you want the rainbow,
you gotta put up with the rain.

—Dolly Parton

This book was originally prepared as a gift for my wife, Fran, and for our family and friends on the happy occasion of our fiftieth anniversary. It is a testament to *love, friendship* and *stamina*. Our fifty years together have encompassed many moments of both rapture and rage. My personal preference is *rapture*.

They said "it wouldn't last." Fran was eighteen when we were married in 1951. From early childhood, music was the dominant interest in her life. She performed on the *Uncle Jack's Kiddie Hour* at five years old, and at eleven was enrolled into the Peabody Preparatory School of Music. Recognized as a gifted young singer, Fran was auditioned by Romano Romani, the voice coach of Rosa Ponselle. Unfortunately, her parents could not afford the cost of private lessons. Fran received her classical music training at the Peabody Conservatory of Music.

Her interests shifted to popular music, and she was invited to sing on the *Ted Mack Talent Show* in New York in 1949, where she won a week's engagement at the Hippodrome Theater in Baltimore. Fran also acted in professional Summer Stock at the Hilltop Theater, and was invited by director George Schaefer to come to New York to study for the musical stage.

When her parents, Bess and Harry, envisioned their young seventeen-year-old daughter living alone in New York—associating with *those crazies* in show business—they

Love requires respect and friendship as well as passion, because there comes a time when you have to get out of bed.

Erica Jong

panicked. At that moment, I happened on the scene, a Johns Hopkins student in love with their talented and beautiful daughter—and a solution to their dilemma.

We were married in 1951 in a ceremony that was almost canceled when Fran locked herself in the bathroom and, for a while, refused to come out. After the wedding festivities, as we left on our honeymoon, my Army Reserve unit was activated for service in the Korean War.

In 1953 we started a family, and Fran was busy tending to three active boys, Jamie, Scott and Adam, while I traveled around the country trying to build sales for my family's packaging business.

Problems developed. Fran had devoted much of her formative years preparing for a career in music. Suddenly, those dreams were squashed; instead she was married, doing dirty diapers and cleaning. After reading a newspaper announcement, she auditioned and obtained a leading role in the musical *Kismet*, produced by The Baltimore Actor's Theater.

Shortly thereafter, Fran was invited to play Jenny in *Three Penny Opera* at Theater Hopkins; the lead role, Vera, opposite Harold Lang in *Pal Joey* at Ford's Theater; and was hired to sing regularly at the newly opened Prime Rib Restaurant and the Roosevelt Bar, a local jazz club.

Fran was hip, and I was square. People said, "It'll never last." It wasn't easy. I learned to understand her needs, as well as respect her talents. Over the years Fran has successfully employed those talents as a poet, singer, and commercial actress, performing over seven hundred radio commercials and jingles. In addition, she managed a home, a family, started a retail chain called The Paper Warehouse, and was one of the principal founders of Baltimore's Center Stage theater.

Friendship. It's not lack of love, but lack of friendship that makes marriages unhappy. My wife, Fran, and I share a deep friendship. Our abiding fondness for each other has been the bonding agent of our relationship. Life together has had its portions of hating and loving; financial abundance and bankruptcy; therapy and marriage encounter; heart catherizations and disabilities; family joys and disappointments.

From a vantage point of fifty years of marriage, I believe we all need to try and laugh more—including the ability to laugh at ourselves. Except for rare life-and-death matters, not everything is as important as it first seems. In my research and experience, the three major challenges that married couples face are money, sex, and communication.

Money. I'm a Libra. Libras aren't good with money. My wife handles the money. She's good at that. I wash the dishes, I'm good at that.

Norman Mailer wrote about marriage, "It all comes down to who does the dishes." That's from someone who had six wives, and stabbed the second. Hah! Confucius said, "Man who sink into woman's arms soon have arms in woman's sink." But I think Robert Middlemiss in his book, *A Common Glory,* got it right when he wrote, "Manhood doesn't wash off in dishwater." Thanks, Bob.

Sex. As for sex, it's a little embarrassing to say, but our love life can be characterized as *fast and furious.* I'm sort of fast, and it makes Fran furious. I probably won't spend a lot of time on that subject.

I *can,* however, say from personal experience that it sometimes helps to use mechanical devices to stimulate arousal in a wife. Chief among these was a 1960 white Mercedes Benz 250 C.

Communication. I have witnessed screaming, yelling, pouting, nagging, whining, moping, blaming, rage, depression, panic and other dysfunctional behaviors—and they have helped Fran and me create a more loving relationship. I understand that a wife needs certain things to make her happy. She needs to be loved, pampered, romanced, wanted, cherished, sought-after and flattered.

It also wouldn't hurt to provide sympathy, devotion, adulation, understanding, and idolatry. That isn't too much to remember, is it?

A Japanese proverb goes, "A joke is often the hole through which the truth whistles." I hope this book will set off some whistles for *you*. People need to laugh more. Having a sense of humor makes it easier to resolve problems and conflicts that will occur in *every* relationship. But if you want the rainbow, you gotta put up with the rain.

Promises, promises

I never promised you
a smile
or taste of me
with your morning coffee
Wherever, Whenever.

I did however,
promise you
rainbows and lilacs
out of season
and Time, Time love,
to grow old with you.

I never promised
to graft my flesh
to yours
and live inside your head
Whenever, Wherever.

I did, however
promise you
a song,
and Time, Time love,
to grow old with you.

— Fran Mahr, 1974

I

Acceptance

If you want the rainbow
you gotta put up with the rain

#1   For richer, for poorer.

Paste a copy of these marriage vows on your refrigerator, pal. There's nothing else in life that you promise "till death do you part." "For poorer" means for poorer. "In sickness" isn't limited to tennis elbow. What part of the promise don't you understand? You have to make relationships work. Relationships don't work by themselves.

Ben White, *The 100 Best Ways to Stay Together*

Life is like an onion, you peel it one layer at a time and sometimes you cry.

Carl Sandburg

I have a good sense of humor, but it wasn't a laughing matter the night in 1993 when I realized my packaging company was headed for bankruptcy. I sat in an empty bathtub in a hotel in Orlando, Florida, and cried.

The bank had been uncooperative with potential buyers. We factored our inventory and accounts receivable, and as a result, we were forced into Chapter 11, into the tender mercies of the greedy lawyers; and the unavoidable closing of a seventy-five-year- old business, of which I was CEO. The bankruptcy occurred "on my watch." I was traumatized, knowing three hundred decent people would be out of work—including me—at age 65.

I've heard the expression, "It hurts too much to laugh and I'm too old to cry"...but I cried anyway in that stupid bathtub in Florida.

And how did my wife, Fran, handle the news? "I'm sorry this happened to you, honey," she said. "I love you and have faith in you. We will get through this *together*."

There is a meaningful Chinese proverb: "My house burnt down, but now I can see the moon." I had the unique opportunity to "see the moon" and realize how fortunate I *really* was, blessed with a loving wife, three supportive sons, and dear friends.

Starting a second career.

I took an advertising course and started a *new* career in Yellow Pages Consulting. My first appointment was with a paint company in downtown Washington. Not wanting to be late, I left early for my 10 A.M. meeting. On the way, two tractor trailers collided, dumping hazardous waste materials over the Baltimore-Washington Parkway. Traffic was rerouted. I arrived late. The owner seemed friendly but extremely pale. As I started my presentation, he interrupted, saying, "I can't follow you anymore. I feel faint. I just had a triple bypass operation, and I've been here since 7 A.M. I'm going home. GOODBYE."

My next appointment was with a hauling and excavating contractor in Sykesville, Maryland. The owner's wife, Lorraine, greeted me with her infant daughter in her arms. We sat at the kitchen table and I gave my forty-minute presentation. Lorraine liked me a lot, but couldn't sign anything without her husband's OK. Luckily Herb drove up, and I repeated everything. Her husband listened carefully.

Make the most of every failure. Fall forward.

Anonymous

"I've got all the fuck'n business I can handle now," he said, eyeing Lorraine and me suspiciously.

I steered the conversation to his plans for growth. Herb informed me that with the cost of equipment, insurance, medical health plans and *what all*, he had no plans to grow. He thought his Yellow Pages ad should even be smaller. I offered to handle the resizing for him. "Why can't Lorraine just call the phone company and find out what a smaller ad costs? Thanks for coming, goodbye."

That was the beginning of my Yellow Pages consulting career. I was discouraged and discussed the situation with my brother-in-law, Ed. He's in sales. Ed really made me feel a lot better by saying, "It only gets worse!"

Then business started to improve. I got a new client, Schafer's Roll Off Service, Inc., a trash removal company. My suggestion to the owner was an ad headline that read:

Your Garbage is Our Bread and Butter

Mrs. Schaffer looked at me quizzically and asked how long had I been creating Yellow Pages ads. We settled on more conservative copy, and I wrote my first contract.

It is only in winter that the pine and cyprus are known to be evergreen.
Confucius

"Refuse Removal" ads became my calling. I soon added Propst Refuse Service and Lowery's Trash Removal to my expanding rubbish, garbage and trash removal client base. I also displayed a natural knack for writing Pest Control ads and developed an unhealthy interest in termites, rodents, roaches, fleas, ticks, mosquitoes, ants, bugs and other pests. This previously hidden talent resulted in my being invited to speak at the National Pest Control Association annual meeting in Nashville.

In my previous, pre-bankruptcy days in the packaging business, I frequently worked odd hours at my desk at home. If Fran saw me working at 3 or 4 o'clock in the morning, she would glare and say, "Go to bed, you're becoming compulsive." In my *new* career, and in our new financial situation, when Fran passed by me on her way to the bathroom in the early hours, I'd say, "Honey, if I get this new ad contract, we can go back to the Prime Rib for dinner."

"Can I make you strong Colombian espresso?" she offered. After several years of creating Yellow Pages ads for clients in a wide variety of businesses, I wrote a book entitled *How to Win in the Yellow Pages*. With a five-star rating on Amazon.com, the book led to more speaking engagements. I was now introduced as "One of America's leading Yellow Pages consultants." I owe it all to garbage, trash, bugs and insects.

Only in America.

2   In sickness and in health.

The sunken moon returns,
the broken branch grows back.
He who ponders this
is not troubled in adversity.

Buddhist proverb

In 1994, a few days after a botched retina eye surgery, I developed a painful urinary blockage and was rushed —disheveled and in pain—to the emergency room at Johns Hopkins Hospital. I was wearing warm-up pants, which were removed to insert the catheter. The long warm-up pants couldn't fit over the bag and catheter. Before being discharged, I asked the nurse to shorten my pants and I would still be able to use them for gym shorts.

Fran provided her own warm-up pants alteration consulting opinion. Using large emergency room shears, the nurse snipped away the cloth and helped me dress. When I glanced down, there were no shorts, only ragged-edged culottes. I looked pitiful: unshaven, hunched over, holding the urine bag, wearing a black eye patch and those damned scraggy culottes. I wanted to *go home.*

As Fran drove into our condominium driveway, I noticed she appeared visibly distressed. I naturally presumed it was a delayed shock reaction from my failed eye surgery followed by my urinary suffering. I patted her arm. "Don't worry, sweetheart, everything's going to be OK."

"Oh, it's not that," she answered. "What if anybody sees me with *you* on the elevator? You look disgusting!"

"OK, I'll use the basement entrance and *crawl* up three

If it weren't for sorrow and bad times, every day would be Christmas.

Lithuanian proverb

flights of stairs so our neighbors won't see us and think we're related." Fran relented. We used the freight elevator.

Onions, smoke, urinary blockages, and women can bring tears to your eyes.

3   Till death do us part.

A man bought his wife a burial plot. The following year he didn't buy her anything and she complained. He answered, "You didn't use the present I bought you last year."

The Beth El Memorial Park in Northwest Baltimore is a well-maintained, stately-looking cemetery with no headstones competing for size and status. Each grave is identified by a similar bronze plaque marker.

It was a bitter cold February day when my dad and I were scheduled to plan the family burial plot arrangements. Fran insisted upon accompanying us. Arriving at the icy cemetery, we were met by a volunteer member of the Memorial Park committee. He said impatiently that he was freezing and wanted to get the arrangements over quickly and go home.

After briefly studying a plot plan, my dad and I said, "Anywhere is OK."

"Just hold on a moment, *please!*" Fran said. "I need to be under a tree."

The volunteer grumbled and located four spots—one resting under a tree. When *that* detail was cleared up, Fran added, "And I also need to be near the road that circles around inside the cemetery."

The irritated volunteer started to protest, but was interrupted. "Near the road or we're not coming here!"

We drove home, secure in the knowledge that Fran would someday rest under a tree and alongside the road. My father laughed, "Fran, why were you so insistent about

Our real grave is not in the ground, but in men's hearts.
Iranian proverb

being positioned near the road and under a tree. What possible difference will any of that mean to you?"

"Well, Dad," she said, "I noticed a Dunkin' Donuts shop just outside the cemetery. My boys can stop for doughnuts and coffee. Then when they come to visit my grave, they can park in the shade—eat their doughnuts, drink their coffee and ENJOY."

"Buzz off, Louise! That was only till death us did part."

II   Communication

If you want empathetic communication, you gotta talk openly about what goes on between you

4   Express your feelings.

*when i can't express
what i really feel
i practice feeling
what i can express
and none of it is equal
i know
but that is why mankind
alone among the mammals
learns to cry*

Nikki Giovanni

Cotton Candy on a Rainy Day (1973)

Feelings are events utilizing the heart. *Thinking* is a rational event exercising the brain, but when your partner *feels* sad, angry, depressed, hurt, unappreciated, or worried, he/she is not usually responsive to logic or reason. Learning how to talk out personal feelings, and be non-judgmental in listening to each other, are valuable attributes for any long-lasting relationship.

The three most important factors in communication are Feelings, Feelings, Feelings.
Doyle Barnett
20 Communication Tips for Couples

We all need somebody to talk to. It would be good if we talked to each other—not just pitter-patter, but real talk…. It's so much easier to be together when we drop our masks.

Liv Ullman

Learning how to stay connected.

"Fran, this is Alice. I'm calling to invite you and Mac to dinner because Gene and I—really love you!"

Fran related the call to me that night, and asked did I think it sounded *strange.* "Strange like in kinky? No!" I said, "Alice is an enthusiastic person."

"You'd best take off your hat and coat and make yourself comfortable, Milton. It's going to be a long, long marriage."

We went to Alice and Gene's home for dinner. The table was set formally with candles and fine china. Their daughters, Karen, Geri, and Leslie, were not at home. As we were seated, Gene poured wine and said, "We wanted you here tonight because we love you. After dinner we're taking you to meet some people who will show you how to really love."

Fran kicked my shins hard under the table. My leg was growing numb. I wondered, "What the hell *is* going on?" In the dark recesses of my mind, the word *orgy* slowly formed. I'm a Libra, so, *on the one hand,* I was feeling uncomfortable. *On the other hand*, I was curious.

As we arrived at our destination, my fantasies were instantly dispelled. The women were young and attractive, many wearing granny dresses. The environment was more like a church social than a swinging disco. Plus, they served a strange-tasting non-alcoholic punch. Yuck. We were warmly welcomed to a Marriage Encounter indoctrination evening. It was explained how the program would help us identify our feelings and teach us to express these feelings to our partner. And to learn how to really love.

Marriage Encounter was started in Spain by the Catholic Church, then imported to North America, where the divorce rates, even among Catholics, were reaching epidemic proportions.

The goals of the forty-eight hour program were to learn how to remove the barnacles that have become encrusted on the hulls of our relationships, and to learn how to become more empathetic with our partners. In so doing, we would develop better techniques of communication, and healthier marriages.

If the bread in the oven is a failure, you lose a week; if the harvest is a failure, you lose a year; if the marriage is a failure, you lose a life.

Estonian proverb

When Fran heard all that business about "expressing feelings," she said "let's try it," and we signed up for a date in January.

Some months later, Fran reminded me that the following weekend was our scheduled Marriage Encounter weekend at Manresa, a Catholic retreat near Annapolis, Maryland.

"Hold on, Fran," I said, "next weekend is Super Bowl. We sure as hell aren't spending Super Bowl in a Catholic retreat."

"But Mac, Alice and Gene will be upset if we don't go."

"Listen, Fran, instead of a marriage encounter, I'll make reservations at the Hilton Hotel in Annapolis. We'll go out Saturday night for dinner. Sunday we'll have a romantic brunch and then watch the Super Bowl game. At 5 o'clock we'll call Alice and Gene and tell them we really, really love them too. It will be a sensational weekend. Doesn't that sound great, sweetheart?"

Off we went to Marriage Encounter. Starting with low conflict issues in our life and marriage, we followed a program alternating group instruction with private sharing time. As instructed, we started expressing feelings in writing, then talking openly and candidly with each other, practicing being empathetic and non-judgmental. We were counseled to write about serious subjects, occasionally striking a raw nerve. One recommended subject was "What are the reasons for going on being with you?" Fran wrote:

In a successful marriage, there is no such thing as one's way. There is only the way of both, only the bumpy, dusty, difficult but always mutual path.
Phyllis McGinley
Pulitzer Prize winner

January 17, 1974

Dear Mac:

I want to make you laugh; I want to make you cry. I want to please you. I want to make you angry. I want to watch you enjoy my delectable gourmet dishes. I want to hear your familiar whistle when you come home after a day's work.

I want to call you on the phone during the day and bug you while your office is full of men and business talk. I want to walk on a cold lonely beach with you and act silly. I want to lie with you under the weight of the blankets and snuggle up and put my icy feet between your legs. I want to use your razor and forget to tell you and have you scream at me as the blood trickles down your chin.

I want to be with you when bad times come to you in your life. I want to be able to help you through them. I want to have parties with you and spend hours afterward talking about the people there. I want to further explore with you my confusion about God. I want to complain to you when I have an ache in my body or my brain. I want to be with you when the downstairs shower completely disintegrates and I can say, "I told you so."

I want to be with you when you hurt. I want to be with you on the day you stop popping Gelusil. I want you to be near me when my loved ones leave this earth. I want to be old with you. I want to live for the time when we can spend days or weeks or months together, doing things, sometimes alone, but always together.

Very important, I want to be me, my own person. I feel so happy. Let's never forget this weekend. Let's help each other carry this feeling with us as we travel home and through life. We really have to do it together.

Suddenly it doesn't feel so cold in this tiny room right now. I can feel your warmth and love. I hope it goes on forever. But no more hoping. Working is the answer. And working with you toward an even better marriage is so much to look forward to.

Your best friend
Fran

On Sunday, the Marriage Encounter experience ended. We repeated our marriage vows before a Catholic priest. He said it was OK—his Boss was Jewish. We wiped back a few tears as everyone held hands and sang:

To love a person is to learn the song in their heart and to sing it to them when they have forgotten.
Thomas Chandler

There is always someone
for each of us they say
And you'll be my someone
forever and a day
I could search the whole world over
until my life is through
And I know I'll never find another you.

We rushed to a pay phone and made two calls. The first was to Alice and Gene to thank them for introducing us to Marriage Encounter. The second was to my wife's oldest friend.

"Frannie, this is Fran. I'm calling to invite you and Sam to dinner because Mac and I—really love you!"

5   If you can't say it—write it!

*The first love letters are
written with the eyes.*
French proverb

The Love Letter Technique. We learned at Marriage Encounter that if talking about your feelings is difficult for you, it helps if you write them out. Writing allows you to *listen* to the voice of your own emotions and will make you feel better for having gotten them off your chest in a mature manner. The most positive communication is a Love Letter.

In his best-selling book, *Men Are from Mars, Women Are from Venus,* John Gray explains the Love Letter Technique. He says by writing your feelings in a prescribed manner, the negative emotions automatically lessen and the positive feelings increase. A Love Letter should express five feelings: **anger, sadness, fear, regret, and love.**

A Love Letter seeking "Understanding."

Dear Fran,
(Anger) I feel you don't understand me and respect the work I do. I hate it when you call me at the office with so-called emergencies. When you called and said the yard was filled with copperhead snakes and our son Adam's life was in danger, I had no choice but to leave my new blonde secretary—who was taking very important dictation—and to head home.

(Sadness) I am sad you can't handle these situations and call at the drop of a hat. You called the day Scott ran away, you called when Jamie was taken to the hospital, and now you bother me about poisonous snakes.

(Fear) I am afraid of snakes. I was raised in the city. I stopped on the way home at a gun store and bought a twenty-two caliber rifle and bullets so I could shoot the little buggers. I bought the gun because I was afraid I wouldn't be good enough to handle the problem without a firearm, and you wouldn't respect me.

(Regret) When I got near the house I heard noises, laughing, the clinking of glasses, and arrived to find you had invited all the neighbors to a "kill the snake" party. Furthermore, someone had already fashioned a loop from a wire hanger, had snared the two baby snakes, and killed them.

(Love) I love you. I want you to be happy. I know you were upset about the snakes and the safety of Adam. Thank you for being my wife. I love you so much. But now that I have the gun, I feel very macho. Maybe I'll get a dog, a cap, a pickup truck and we can drive around the neighborhood drinking beer and shooting snakes.

Love, Bubba

"My wife doesn't understand me."

A Love Letter about "Indifference."

Dearest Fran,
(Anger) I am angry about your going to sing at the
Roosevelt Bar last Saturday on the back of Frank's
motorcycle and not coming home until 2 A.M. I'm upset
that I had to explain to the kids that Mom wouldn't be
home for dinner, and that they would have to fix it
themselves.

(Sadness) I am sad because I feel you are indifferent to me and don't care about me the way I care about you. It's true that I go to Europe and Asia to buy machinery, and I travel frequently by myself to Puerto Rico, Palm Springs, New Orleans and other exciting cities around the country to call on retailers and distributors, but that's business.

(Fear) I am afraid that what my friend, Bob, says is true. That you will run off with one of those hippie musicians, and leave me alone with all three boys. You know I can't stand their constant bickering.

(Regret) I feel embarrassed when the kids keep asking why their friends' mothers prepare breakfasts, but when they knock on your door you yell, "What do think I am, your slave? What are you trying to do, kill me?" I explain that you are in show business and are a night person. I am sorry not to have looked on the bright side, which is that the boys now know how to cook gourmet Italian dishes for dinner.

(Love) I love you. I understand that you need to do your own thing. I forgive you. I feel so lucky to have you in my life. The boys are making my favorite, *chicken cacciatore* with *cheerios,* tonight.

Love, Mac

A Love Letter about "Arguing."

Dear Fran:

(Anger) I am angry when you get so emotional. I am upset that you keep misunderstanding me. I am angry that you are so sensitive and easily hurt. You prepared a great dinner last weekend in Ocean City. I loved it, the kids loved it, and both Jean and Burt loved it. After dinner when you were cleaning up the dirty pots and pans, and Burt was walking the kids on the beach, it was nice of Jean to get out her guitar and start singing sultry French love songs as I lay stretched out on the sofa.

(Sadness) I know you were doing the dishes, but I am sad that you took offense when I asked you to "hold down the racket 'cause Jean was singing." It hurt to see you angry and to feel you didn't love me. I know you felt a little unhappy with the attention I was paying to Jean. She is sexy, talented, beautiful, and has a great figure. But so what?

(Fear) I am afraid that whatever I do will upset you. When you came into the room and asked me sweetly did I want some red wine, and when I said yes, you poured the whole decanter on my head. That wasn't nice.

(Regret) I am sorry if I hurt you and my words were insensitive. You don't deserve to be treated that way. I'm also sorry you used red wine, because the stains won't come out of my shirt or the sofa.

(Love) I love you. I think I can listen to your feelings now. This time when we talk, I will be more patient and understanding. You deserve that.

Love, Mac

P.S. Do you have Jean's phone number?

6 Avoid a simple discussion turning into an argument.

"If something is bothering you about our relationship, Lorraine, why don't you just spell it out."

A "Dictionary of Relationship Talk" outlined in the book *We Can Work It Out,* by Clifford Notarius and Howard Markman, identifies self-defeating patterns of discussion. By reviewing these examples, you will no longer be mystified by how a simple discussion can turn into an argument.

Examples of "Dictionary of Relationship Talk":

Positive problem point. (Any statement that gives information about the nature of a problem. It should not be yelled, whined, or blurted out.)

>   Fran: *"The garbage needs to be taken out."*

Negative problem talk. (Gives problem information in a nasty voice.)

>   Fran: *"Take out the damn trash, now! If it's not too much trouble?"*

Excuses and delays. (A response that tries to justify a desired action.)

>   Mac: *"I can't take out the trash now, I'm watching 'Everybody loves Raymond.'"*

Positive solution talk. (Any response that offers a reasonable solution.)

>   Mac: *"I'll take out the trash as soon as this program is over."*

Negative solution talk. (A statement that is unreasonable or unrealistic.)

>   Mac: *"If it's that important, do it yourself."*

Mind-reading talk. (A presumption of what your partner is thinking.)

>   Fran: *"You don't care if we have bugs or mice. You never do anything I ask without my having to get hysterical. I think you must enjoy that!"*

Critical talk. (A remark that criticizes your partner.)

> Fran: *"After all the things I do for you, I don't understand how you can be so disagreeable and inconsiderate."*

Listening talk. (Any comment that shows your partner that you heard her and understood what she was trying to say.)

> Mac: *"I guess you're upset about the trash not being taken out."*

Agreement. (A comment that agrees with your wife.)

> Mac: *"You're right. You are a caring and considerate person."*

Disagreement. (A remark that implies disagreement.)

> Mac: *"I think you're overreacting to a stupid thing like taking out trash. What's really bothering you?"*

Hopeless talk. (A statement that expresses pessimism about the problem, the partner or the relationship.)

> Fran: *"I should have married Maynard."*

#7 Listen, Listen, Listen.

*A man has two ears
and one mouth: he
therefore should listen
more than he talks.*
Danish proverb

*The power of empathetic listening is the power to transform
relationships. Without being listened to, we are shut up in the
solitude of our own hearts.*
Michael P. Nichols
The Lost Art of Listening, Guilford Press (1995)

*"I do think your problems are serious, Richard.
They're just not very interesting."*

The first duty of love is to listen.
Paul Tillich

Most people don't listen with the intent to *understand;* they listen with the intent to *reply*. My mother-in-law's favorite response is, "That's nothing."

"That's nothing, she said, interrupting me, "let me tell you what happened last week. I stored my Yellow Pages book in the oven and set the place on fire. The fire engines came and the whole nursing home was evacuated. It was the most fun I've had all year."

Inattentive listening:
When we are not listening with the intent to really understand, or to put ourselves in the other person's shoes.

"Don't worry."
(Translation: "Your problems are not so serious.")

Fran's grandmother, Mary, was visiting her brother-in-law Morris in a hospital after his painful prostate surgery. As poor Morris was describing his agony, Mary interrupted, "Oy Morris,...I know, I had it too."

"You shouldn't feel that way."
(Translation: "I don't want to hear about your problems.")

Mel was recommended by our building manager. He said he could repair the sliding glass doors for a low, low price and could start immediately.

"Please be careful," Fran implored him, "this apartment has just been freshly painted, and I would appreciate it if you are careful and don't make a mess."

"Yes ma'am," answered low bidder Mel.

He and his helper started chipping away concrete from the door frame in order to make the balcony opening a little wider. The wind off the ocean picked up and blew the concrete dust inside, coating the entire apartment. Everything was covered with a chalky-white substance: walls, floors, furniture.

When confronted with the mess, Mel smiled and said, "Nobody's perfect." Fran bitterly complained to the building manager.

"Don't be upset," he said, "have a good cry, you'll feel better."

The cleanup cost was deducted from Mel's bill. Mel was no longer smiling. As he left he commented, "These condo units are easy to break into. You just have to know how to lift the door off the tracks. Have a nice day."

Seek first to understand, than to be understood.
Francis of Assisi

Empathetic listening.

When you let your partner understand you are actively listening by giving feedback or echoing. Echoing rephrases what your spouse has told you. It gives your partner the chance to further clarify if necessary.

"I think I understand you correctly."

"Let me get this straight, Fran. Once we're married I can't sleep with anyone else for the rest of my life, and if things don't work out you get half of everything I own. I think I understand you correctly. Could I mull it over and get back to you?"

"I want to be certain I understand what you mean."

Tom was recommended by a sarcastic salesgirl in a fabric store in Fort Pierce, who—after Fran had said her prices were too high for the third time—suggested we try the place across the railroad tracks on Farmers Market Road, and there we met Tom.

Stripped to the waist, wearing a sheepherder's hat in a building with no air conditioning and one hundred degree temperature, the upholsterer told us he was completely backed up with work for the next six weeks.

It was unbearable in his workshop. I went outside to wait in our air-conditioned car. Five minutes later, I heard live guitar music and Fran singing. The upholstery was now magically going to be finished within 24 hours.

As we drove away, Tom hollered, "Now Fran darlin...don't mess with ma heart."

Fran waved and responded, "I'll be in touch, Tom."

"In touch," I repeated, puzzled. "I'm trying to improve my listening skills with empathy and feedback. I want to be certain I understand what you meant when you said to that guy, "I'll be in touch."

"I invited Tom and his family for dinner Saturday night. We're going to have a country music jam session."

"Sorry I asked."

8   Avoid "I-Can't-Stand-It-Itis."

I-Can't-Stand-It-Itis is a condition reflecting a person's tendency to view common inconvenient or annoying situations as unbearable.

> Henry was stunned to come home from work to find his wife stuffing all her belongings into a suitcase.
>
> "What on earth are you doing?" he cried.
>
> "I can't stand it anymore!" she shrieked. "Thirty-two years we've been married, and all we do is bicker and quarrel and ignore each other. I'm leaving!"
>
> Stunned, Henry watched his wife close the suitcase, lug it down the stairs, and proceed to walk out of the house, out of his life. Suddenly he was galvanized into action. Running into the bedroom and grabbing a second suitcase, he yelled back at his wife, "Sylvia, you're right, you're absolutely right — and I can't bear it either. Wait a minute, and I'll go with you."

The bald-headed man will not grow hair by getting excited.
Chinese proverb

Sometimes my wife exhibits symptoms of I-Can't-Stand-It-Itis. I said, "Honey, I read something interesting in a motorcycle maintenance magazine while I was getting the oil changed in the gas station. You may be experiencing a condition called I-Can't-Stand-It-Itis. That's when a person has a low frustration tolerance, and irrationally believes that they must always get what they want easily and without effort. And if not—they can't stand it."

"Don't bother me. Can't you see I'm paying bills?" Fran responded irritably.

"Further, precious," I continued, "I–Can't–Stand–It–Itis also means that your husband or sons must never do or say anything you don't like because that would make you feel annoyed or uncomfortable. "An example," I patiently explained, "is asking you time and time again to do my laundry. When I said black underwear turns me on, I didn't mean you shouldn't wash my shorts for a month. Do you understand my message, angel?"

"Mac darling," Fran replied, "up yours."

9   Be less critical.

I tell you one thing—
If you want peace of mind,
do not find fault with others.
Sri Sarada Deci (1836–86)

"When will he be able to sit up and take criticism?"

Criticism is the adult version of crying for attention.

In *The Lost Art of Listening,* published by Guilford Press (1995), Michael P. Nichols explains that our parents may be the most important unfinished business in our lives. A husband who shuts his ears when he feels criticized by his wife might discover a part of himself that feels like a little boy expecting to be reprimanded. Even if his wife is trying to express her loneliness and need for him, if she speaks critically, it may recall memories of parental disapproval and control.

My mother came to this country when she was eight months old. She never got beyond a sixth grade education before she went to work as a ribbon clerk in Hutzlers, a local department store. There was no Oprah, Dr. Spock, TV, or talk radio to teach her how to parent. I learned early on that criticism can sting and unjust criticism can be damaging.

My rebelliousness created unwanted tensions in the family, and at age fourteen I was shipped off to military school. I couldn't understand my mother's critical behavior or recognize the love that hid behind it.

Unfortunately, many years were wasted before I realized mother had difficulty expressing her love. She suffered with Parkinson's Disease, and a few months before her tragic death, by drowning in her bathtub at age eighty-four, she wrote in her shaky handwriting:

Honest criticism is hard to take, particularly from a relative, a friend, an acquaintance, or a stranger.
Franklin P. Jones

Dear Malcolm,

It never occurred to me that the boy we had would bring me so much pleasure. You and your wife are very dear to me. My pleasure is being close to you.
A little late, but this is for every day of my life.
       All my Love,
        Mom

Few of us are Mother Teresa. It isn't easy, when we're being unfairly trashed, to suspend self concern. Those fearful parts of us, once triggered, can reduce us to childhood insecurity and the anxiety that accompanies it. Criticism need not be a stressful or guilt-producing event. We all make mistakes. Where criticism *is* justified, acknowledge it. If it's unwarranted bullshit, ignore it.

How to take criticism without overreacting.
Other than therapists, there are other practitioners who may help you learn how to take criticism without overreacting. One technique I am personally familiar with is called Bull Baiting.

Bull Baiting is based upon the psychological theory of waving a red flag in front of a bull to incite him, then conditioning people not to overreact in the face of criticism.

I discussed the program with Fran and we signed up. At the appointed time, two Bull Baiters arrived at our home, explaining they were sent from the Church of Scientology to conduct the Bull Baiting program. Their technique, they explained, was to work with us, one- on-

one, saying uncomfortable things to us and building up in intensity. We would learn to manage the criticism which would be applied in ever-increasing dosages. The expected result was that no matter what anyone ever said to us in the future, we would be totally immune to criticism.

As we started, the leader, a good-looking young woman, reminded me these exercises required my complete concentration. She looked me in the eyes and said, "You have a big nose."

I giggled. "Please," chided the pretty lady, "be serious."

"And you also have funny looking ears," she said.

With that comment, I became hysterical. I didn't look at Fran because I knew my laughter would be contagious.

"I wish you would stop fooling around," she said critically.

She tried once again. "The separation between your teeth looks like Bugs Bunny."

That did it. I was totally out of control—shaking with laughter—tears rolling down my cheeks. I was told I failed the course—Fran failed too.

You have to give those people from the The Church of Scientology credit. She offered to bring their minister to meet us, so we could consider converting, joining, and contributing to the Church of Scientology.

We thanked them and said we were very happy with our current religious affiliation for the present, but if we changed our minds we would get back to them.

I still don't handle criticism very well, but now I can see red flags without overreacting. Olé.

Talking about bulls is altogether different than being in the arena.
Spanish proverb

#10   To thine own self be true.

This above all: to thine own self be true,
and it must follow, as the night the day,
thou canst not then be false to any man.
William Shakespeare
Hamlet, Act 1, Sc.3

We know the story. One December evening in 1955 a woman left work in Montgomery, Alabama and boarded a bus for home. She was tired; her feet ached. As the bus became crowded, the woman, a black woman, was ordered to give up her seat to a white passenger. When Rosa Parks remained seated, her simple decision led to the bus boycott led by Martin Luther King, Jr., and the eventual disintegration of institutionalized segregation in the South.

Four years *earlier,* during the Korean War, we lived in Columbus, Georgia. I was attending the Infantry School at nearby Fort Benning. Fran was eighteen years old.

Race relations in Georgia were little different than in neighboring Alabama. One morning Fran was riding on a fully- loaded bus in Columbus, with all the white folk sitting in the front and all the black folk seated in the rear.

Onto the bus stepped a frail old black lady with a cane and a large shopping bag. Fran, out of respect for the woman's age, immediately rose and offered her seat. The lady smiled, sadly shaking her head. Fran insisted the elderly woman take her place. Hostile stares, sneers and ugly racial slurs were directed at Fran by a few of the white passengers. Eighteen-year-old Fran, frightened, but resolute, remained standing until the aged woman reached her destination.

What you are shouts
so loud I cannot hear
what you are saying.
Ralph Waldo Emerson

When the film *Amistad* was released in 1997, the *Stuart News*, a Florida newspaper, published a letter to the editor urging the movie not be shown in local theaters.

Entitled, "Give it a rest. No need to stir passions with films about slavery," the writer noted: "Slavery is evil and immoral, but no one living in America today was alive or responsible for the practice of slavery in the U.S. Yet films and TV continue to inflame passions with productions showing the cruelty of slavery. Steven Spielberg's *Amistad* is a good example. *Amistad* stirs up resentment between the races. Give it a rest."

Fran was incensed by the article in the *Stuart News*. Her response was published:

Editor:

In response to the article, 'Give it a rest' on Feb. 21, of course slavery is evil and immoral. So was the Holocaust where six million Jews were killed. So are all the persecutions and killing of innocent people in Oklahoma City, Bosnia, Algeria, South Africa, Ireland and around the world. And finally, so is the victimization of people who have chosen gay or lesbian lifestyles.

Digging a hole in the beautiful Treasure Coast sand, and putting one's head in it, accomplishes nothing. We need more films like *Amistad, Schindler's List, La Cage aux Folles* and *Philadelphia* to educate people to life's past and present realities: to help us understand and respect people who are different in skin color, religion, sexual preference and ethnic background.

Deeds are fruits,
words are only leaves.
Greek proverb

Most current films are filled with death, destruction, ugly violence or delightful foolishness. When high-quality films are produced that encourage understanding between people with different backgrounds or lifestyles, we should welcome the opportunity to view them, and encourage our friends and families to profit from the experience as well. Let's never give hate, ignorance, greed and bigotry a rest.

Fran Mahr
Jensen Beach

III   Conflict resolution

If you want to resolve a conflict successfully; you gotta have two winners

I have spent most of my life with you
my friend
my parent
my love
We have
shared
fought
dug
into each other's guts
Sometimes
leaving sutures
to fester
More often
closing the wound
with a kiss
Whatever magic
or mystery
there is to love
I see only you.
— Fran Mahr

Even Buddhist priests
of the same temple
quarrel occasionally.
Sengalese proverb

Almost all married people fight, although many are ashamed to admit it. Fran and I can't be quiet about it because we live in a condominium apartment, and the neighbors hear us.

I'm very intuitive about when a fight is impending. My wife turns the bathroom fans on to deaden the noise, her face darkens, her eyes bulge, her lips curl, and she says between clenched teeth, "We need to talk!"

Many people seem to think that conflict, if ignored, will go away. Not so! If it's serious to your spouse, it's serious.

"It's got to come out, of course, but that doesn't address the deeper problem."

#11 Confront your problems before they confront you.

Many couples carry around emotional baggage, whether an unpleasant event we experienced at work, a problem with our kids, or some unresolved feelings about our mate.

When a new flare-up occurs, the issue left "up-in-the-air" (the baggage) may kick in, leaving us feeling angry, frustrated and wanting to disengage emotionally. If you don't want to talk about something, it's probably something you *should* talk about.

"Stanley, we need to talk, so please don't interrupt."

Former president and international peacemaker Jimmy Carter says he's never won an argument with his wife; and the only times he thought he had, he found the argument wasn't over.

I try to understand.
I've seen you draw away,
and show the pain.
It's hard to know what I can say
to turn things right again,
to have the coolness melt,
to share once more
the warmth we've felt.

Jimmy Carter, *Always a reckoning*

How to confront a problem. If you have a problem to discuss with your partner, though it may be distasteful, confront your problem before it confronts you, even battle over it. But don't fight to win—fight to tie.

EXAMPLE: Key West Florida, 1994, while 300,000 people watch "the mother of all sunsets" from Mallory Square, we are in Pepy's Steak House, because they offer a discounted Early Bird Special.

"Mac, there's something I need to talk about," Fran said. "I'm worried about my mortality."

"Let's not discuss it now, Fran. Enjoy your meal."

"I know you don't want to hear this, but I need you to listen to me— if you can stop stuffing your face for two seconds. It's not death that worries me, it's dying with pain and indignity."

Unresolved problems are fertilized by time.
Doyle Barnet
20 Communication Tips for Couples

When you solve one problem, you keep one-hundred away.
Chinese proverb

"Honey, we're in Key West. We're on vacation. We just missed an incredible sunset—all because you insist on eating at 5:30. So lighten up already."

"I wanted us to eat now to get the early bird. It saves money. Somebody in this family has to worry about finances."

"I know you are concerned about stuff like money and dying, but you're spoiling a lovely evening by being morbid. We only go around once...."

"I don't think I have long to live," she interrupted. "If I can't talk to my husband about serious illness, who can I talk to?"

"My God, are you seriously ill and you haven't told me?"

"No, I'm fine, but when we're dead we're soon forgotten. When I die I want a big funeral, with a tent, and I want you to be sure to invite all my musician friends to a happy celebration of my life. I want everybody to remember me with a smile on my face."

"Dear, a funeral is a casket closing, not a Broadway opening, but I'm glad you got that out of your system."

"If I keep things bottled up inside, it makes me crazy. I feel better when I can share my feelings of death with you."

"Uh huh. Honey, your sirloin steak is loaded with artery-clogging cholesterol. As a loving husband, I'll finish it for you."

12   Know when to call a time-out.

When you are engaged in an argument that's making you feel upset, your body may be responding to a primitive alarm system inherited from our prehistoric ancestors. Your body perceives the situation as dangerous—it responds the same way, whether we are facing a saber- toothed tiger or an angry spouse.

John Gottman
The Seven Principles for Making Marriage Work

The prudent embark when the sea is calm, the rash when it's stormy.
Chinese proverb

"I'm going to New Zealand for a walk."

How to conduct a time-out. When a discussion becomes an argument, and escalates to the point of diminishing returns, it's wise to request a break. A time-out is designed to quiet down the mind, reduce the blood pressure, and allow everyone time to calm down. It is an effective way to break the chain reaction and prevent emotional damage.

No parting shots. When someone calls for a time-out, and the partner agrees, there should be no last zingers.

> *I married you for better or worse...*
> *when does it get better?*

Kindle not a fire you cannot put out.
Chinese proverb

Leave at once. The person calling the time-out should immediately leave the room or the house. A time-out should last for one hour. If it goes longer, people feel abandoned.

After one nasty argument, I took a time-out and flew to Puerto Rico to visit our packaging distributor. Upon arrival at the Jeronimo Hilton in San Juan, eighty incoming guests were sitting uncomfortably on their luggage in the lobby. The Navy League—on a day-tour—had not yet checked out.

My customer said, "This is unacceptable, let me take you to a lovely Spanish hotel in downtown San Juan, El Convento."

I planned to be away for only forty-eight hours, so I didn't advise my wife of the hotel change. Fran tried to reach me at the Jeronimo Hilton. She learned that I never checked in and became concerned. Fran called her friends

Ellen and Frannie, who gave her the names of other major hotels in San Juan. When I wasn't found registered at any of these hotels either, concern became suspicion.

Her friends helped by saying, "All men are scum." The next day, I was sitting in the offices of M. Badrena & Sons. Señor Badrena was also the Papal Nuncio of Puerto Rico.

The telephone rang. Señor Badrena announced the long distance call was for me. I nervously picked up the receiver and got an earful from my precious wife—stateside.

"You are a miserable, unfaithful bastard," she screamed. "Mother's taking the children. Ellen is driving me to the airport. I'm coming to San Juan!" The phone slammed down with a bang.

I put my hand over the receiver and said, "It's my wife, she misses me, and has decided to join me here in San Juan."

"Ah, how romantic," Señor Badrena said, and he had flowers sent to our room in the El Convento.

Hot heads and cold hearts never solved anything.
Anonymous

3 Always return when your time is up. Failing to come back from a time-out only makes things worse. Your partner will feel rejected and may consider contacting a lawyer, who will be happy to arrange for your total economic and marital destruction.

4 Don't use drugs or alcohol during time-out. You have enough problems already, you don't need drugs. Alcohol will exacerbate angry feelings or reduce your inhibitions.

A husband returns home very late from a time-out. As he undresses, his wife sees that he doesn't have his jockey shorts. She asks, "Where's your underwear?"

The man looks down and says, "My God, I've been robbed."

5 Do something relaxing. The best thing to do during a time-out is to take a walk, practice meditation, listen to music, or exercise to release endorphins into your bloodstream to help you calm down.

A psychologist told his patient to walk five miles a day to release stress. After two weeks the patient called in. The psychologist said, "Well, how are things at home?" The patient replied, "How should I know? I'm 70 miles away."

6 Check in when you get back. Do not use the time-out to sweep things under the rug. Start the conversation with: "I know that I was partly responsible for the argument." This approach permits both parties to reexamine the issues without defensiveness. Marriage isn't easy. Sometimes even a long time-out doesn't work.

Marriage is the roughest thing in the world. Nelson Mandela endured twenty-seven years in a South African prison. But once he got out, it only took two years before his marriage busted his ass.

Chris Rock

When you shoot an arrow of truth, dip the point in honey.

Arabian proverb

#13 Men and women differ genetically.

Have you ever felt that when you argue with your wife, she seems to calm down faster, and you're still left with angry, stressful feelings? Anthropologists tell us that this difference lies in gene programming, our evolutionary heritage, based on surviving in a harsh environment. According to John Gottman, in *The Seven Principles for Making Marriage Work*, "Women, particularly nursing mothers, calmed down quickly after stress. This was because the amount of milk produced was affected by how relaxed they felt, related to the release of the hormone oxytocin to the brain. By remaining composed, she enhanced her children's opportunity for survival by optimizing the amount of nutrition received."

For the male it was the opposite. For the early hunters, vigilance was a key survival skill. So males whose adrenalin kicked in quite readily and who did not calm down so easily were more likely to survive and procreate. To this day the male cardiovascular system remains more reactive than the female and slower to recover from stress.

The man is the flame,
the woman the glow.
Russian proverb

"You may well be from Mars, but the children and I are still from Westchester."

Women are feeling sharers.

Why were you on the phone so long, Fran?

I was talking to Donna.

You are always complaining about our phone bills.

What other pleasures do I have in my life?

What can you possibly have to say that takes an hour?

I don't know. I was telling her about Jamie and she was telling me about C.J. Then I was telling her about my mother and she was telling me about her mother. Then I was telling her about Scott and she was telling me about Tamara. Then I was telling her about Adam and she was telling me about Colette.

You talked to her yesterday, and E-mailed her last night.

Yes, but sharing my feelings is very helpful to me.

You say the same thing about talking to Frannie, Alice, Susan, Marsha, Lennie, Jackie, June, Bev, Barbara, Ellen, Lesley, Muriel, Martine, Flo, Sandy, Alfreda, Betty, Velia, Paula, Mary, Marie, your mother, your sister, and your cousins Roz, Sis, Sylvia and Nicki.

Leave me alone. I've got bills to pay, and I never seem to have time to get everything done. You think I'm superwoman?

Men are problem solvers.
Did you play tennis with Bob today?

Yeah.

Well, what did you two talk about?

I told him I had a tennis elbow problem, but I solved
the problem by using a Tendex mercury wrist band. He
said he had a back problem and fixed it by taking two
Tylenols.

Did he tell you how much he got for selling his business?

No.

Why not?

I didn't ask.

Did he tell you about the Pikeville wedding—that
everybody in town—but us—was invited to?

No.

Why?

We didn't discuss it.

You call that a relationship? You two never talk about
anything really interesting.

Maybe that's why we've remained friends for 55 years.

14   Don't dredge up ancient history

People dredge up ancient history because they have never resolved the original problem. My sons taught me that when you try to dredge up too much old stuff, it makes it difficult to resolve problems. And it can also give you a very nasty headache.

Once, when the boys were young, Fran said, "There they go again, fighting. Please make them stop before I have a stroke."

Don't let yesterday use up too much of today.
Cherokee Indian saying

"You didn't like living in a tree. Now you don't like living in a cave!"

I calmly called the boys together and asked, "What's all this racket, and why is there a hole in our glass front door?"

Jamie said, "Adam threw his ice skates at my head."

"Why did you throw ice skates at Jamie's head, Adam?"

"Because he hit me."

"Why did you hit your little brother, Jamie?"

"Because last week he took my valuable coin collection that Daddy Maurice gave me, and spent it all on cheeseburgers and cokes at Windy Valley."

"Adam, why did you take Jamie's coin collection and.... Oh never mind, the hell with it!"

#15 Pick the right time and place for discussions.

When your man is mad, wait until he's in the right mood. Never approach fire with gas.
Risa Mickenberg
Taxi Driver Wisdom

We may assume that the people we care about will listen to us whenever we feel like talking. But if we realize that good listening doesn't happen automatically, we'll learn to give more thought to finding the right time to approach people.
Michael Nichols
The Lost Art of Listening, Guilford Press (1995)

"Is this a good time to bring up a car problem?"

Michael Nichols advises that problems shouldn't be ignored, but it's important to find the right time and place for partners to be in the mood for discussing them. No matter how much couples care about each other, there are times when one or the other doesn't have the patience, energy or opportunity to listen.

"The other night I said to my wife, 'Do you feel that the sex and excitement has gone out of our marriage?' She said, 'I'll discuss it with you during the next commercial break.'"
Jackie Carter

16   Never go to bed angry.

Phyllis Diller suggests, "Never go to bed angry with your wife. It's better to stay up and fight."

Milton Berle says, "My wife and I have an agreement that we never go to sleep angry with each other. We've been awake now for six months."

Marriage is the only war in which you sleep with the enemy.
Mexican proverb

"What ever happened to 'Never go to bed angry'?"

Anger and intimacy are not good bedfellows. At bedtime when you're having angry feelings, it may feel uncomfortable, but it's better to have disagreements resolved rather than fester overnight.

You might say to your partner, "I want you to know that I respect your feelings, even though I can't agree with everything you're saying. But what's most important is I love you."

By voicing this, you are acknowledging you are not overreacting to the situation, nor are you ignoring it or conceding.

What you are doing is reducing the feelings of anger, and setting the stage for a rational discussion at a more suitable time.

Fran and I rarely go to bed angry or with unresolved problems. Now that I work at home we can fight *any* time.

17   Anger sets the stage for more anger.

When angry, count ten before you speak;
if very angry, a hundred.
Thomas Jefferson
A Decalogue of Canons for Observation in Practical Life (1825)

If you are patient in a
moment of anger, you
will escape a hundred
days of sorrow.
Chinese proverb

You must feed your anger or it will dissipate.
When you get angry, your heart rate and blood pressure go up, your muscles tense, and sugar is released into your bloodstream. You're ready to do battle.

The full heat of emotions is brief, lasting *seconds*, rather than minutes or hours. For an emotion to last longer you must keep feeding it. Anger sets the stage for more anger.

BOOTH

"I've got an idea for a story: Gus and Ethel live on Long Island, on the
North Shore. He works sixteen hours a day writing fiction. Ethel never
goes out, never does anything except fix Gus sandwiches and in the end
she becomes a nympho-lesbo-killer-whore. Here's your sandwich."

Anger repressed can poison a relationship as surely as the cruelest words.
Joyce Brothers

The venting approach. Suppressing anger is like keeping the lid on a pressure cooker. Eventually the steam builds up to the point of explosion.

One useful way of dissipating repressed anger is by positive venting. Venting of your emotions during a conflict is helpful as long as you focus on the problem and not direct it against your spouse in the form of a personal attack.

"Well, who made the magic go out of our marriage—you or me?"

Positive venting. You can vent anger positively by physical exercise (endorphins); by writing down your feelings (love letters); by visualization to dispel anger (It's *just* a bad day, it's not a bad *life*. Be happy; he did a *bad* thing, but he's a *good* person.); or by talking constructively to your partner and expressing your feelings.

"I feel really upset about your opening and reading my mail, Fran. I need to talk about it and get it off my chest. I feel that either you don't trust me to give you the checks that come in, or that you want to control me. Either way, opening someone's mail is a federal offense, punishable by a fine or imprisonment. So in an open, honest and assertive fashion, I am suggesting you stop opening my mail or it's Hasta la vista, baby!"

Negative venting. Negative venting of anger may help maintain your self respect, but it doesn't resolve problems. When you lose your temper, you are no longer in charge of your own anger.

Anyone can become angry— that is easy; but to be angry with the right person, and to the right degree, at the right time, for the right purpose, and in the right way — that is not easy.
Aristotle

A young salesman is driving a car late at night out in the middle of nowhere, and he gets a flat tire. In the trunk there is no jack. He sees a light from a farmhouse half a mile away and starts to walk there, hoping to get a jack and get back on the road. He is angry over this inconvenience. He thinks the farmer will be annoyed to be awakened at this late hour, and will turn him away. The more he obsesses about being rejected, the more his anger builds.

The salesman approaches the house and rings the bell. The farmer answers to the door. "Howdy son, what's the problem? How can I help you?"

Negatively venting his repressed anger, the salesman answers, "Keep your goddam jack!"

18   Don't catastrophize.

When you tell yourself that a given situation or behavior is horrible or awful, you are saying that the situation is the worst thing that could ever happen to you. As long as you keep catastrophizing, you will be exaggerating your problems and be flooded with rage, panic or depression.

Kenneth Wenning, *Men Are From Earth, Women Are From Earth.*

My wife, Fran, catastrophizes. One of her favorites is: after she dies I will remarry, and the new trophy-wife-slut will get everything before our sons do (whose names are already taped under all the furniture and behind our artwork.)

Fear less, hope more; eat less; chew more; whine less; love more; and all good things will be yours.

Swedish proverb

Fran and Madeleine. In 1994 our youngest son, Adam, opened A Mano, an upscale retail store in Georgetown in Washington, D.C., featuring hand-crafted ceramic tableware.

On one occasion Fran and I were visiting Adam, and Clinton's Secretary of State, Madeleine Albright, walked in. Fran was strolling around the store.

I whispered to Adam, "That's Madeleine Albright. Shouldn't you personally greet her?" Adam trained at Brooks Brothers in New York. They have a restrained sales approach. He said to Mrs. Albright, "Hi there, let me know if you need any help."

Fran saw me whispering to Adam, and she *catastrophized*. She thought I was telling him this somewhat rumpled-looking lady was a shoplifter. Fran signaled by raising one finger to her eye and pointing that she would undertake personal surveillance of the suspect.

As Adam and I watched helplessly, Fran sidled next to Mrs. Albright. Standing very close, she gave her the—*over my dead body will you steal from my baby*—stare.

The former Secretary of State, no stranger to adverse situations, volunteered a polite, pinched smile and made a graceful exit. Victorious Fran smiled broadly, giving us the two thumbs-up victory sign.

For some reason, Adam doesn't invite us to his store as much as he used to.

19   Nagging is in the ear of the beholder.

I love being married. It's so great to find that one special person you want to annoy the rest of your life.
Rita Rudner

A lobster loves the water, but not when he's cooked in it.
Sengalese proverb

Fran nags about my driving. She says, "Why must you always tailgate? Please don't talk while you're driving. Did you fill the gas tank? When was the last time you changed the oil? We're not in England, why are you on the left side of the road? Don't speed in a school zone? Look out for those children! Oh my God!"

Make your suggestions sound like requests.
Sometimes people nag trying to improve a partner's behavior. If you recognize that on occasion you *do* nag, consider making your suggestions sound like requests.

> "Mac dear, I would really appreciate it if you didn't leave powder on the bathroom floor. I nearly tripped today and almost fell on my new hip replacement. I know you wouldn't want that on your conscience. Also, love, if you could spare a moment out of your busy schedule to pick up the bath mat and close the shower curtain, I would be ever so grateful, because we don't live in a pig sty."

"They just told me you were paroled three weeks ago! Why won't you come home?"

#20   Words have the power to hurt or heal.

To keep your marriage brimming
With love in the marriage cup,
Whenever you're wrong admit it,
Whenever you're right, shut up.
Ogden Nash

Magical words.

There are two kinds of people in the world: those who come into a room and say, "Here I am!" and those who come and say, "Ah, there you are!"

"If I die first, you should remarry. If you die first, I'll get a dog."

Healing words.

"I'm sorry I upset you. Will you please forgive me?"

Never say "NEVER".... Always avoid "ALWAYS."

Always and *never* are negative words and sweeping generalizations used to describe a partner's behavior.

"You **never** care about my feelings."
"You **always** interrupt me when I'm talking."

Use the word "I" rather than the word "YOU."
Statements starting with "You" can be condemning and make people feel defensive. They are counterproductive. Positive rapport can be accomplished more easily by starting your sentence with "I." This word focuses on how you're feeling rather than accusing your partner.

Don't say: "**You** think I'm your maid."
Say: "**I** really appreciate you helping around the house."

Don't say: "All **you** do is sit in front of that stupid TV."
Say: "**I** would love to spend time alone with you."

Don't say: "**You** should be an earthquake predictor, because **you** can find a fault faster than anyone."
Say: "**I** am interested in your constructive suggestions."

Don't say: "**You** must be from India, you're untouchable."
Say: "Have you lost weight? **I** think you look sexy."

Words are, of course, the most powerful drug used by mankind.
Rudyard Kipling

If you scatter thorns,
don't go barefoot.
Italian proverb

Zingers are nasty little one-liners.
Zingers are used for *put-downs*. They are little verbal land mines that can cause explosive reactions.

> "**If only** I had known that when the cooing stopped the billing would begin."

> "**If only** you paid as much attention to me as you do to Sandy, Donna, Susan, Mary, and 'what's-her-face' on the third floor."

> "**If only** I had known that you were going to complain about being *wanted*, I would have gone to the post office and hung up your picture."

A hero is someone who
can keep his mouth shut
when he is right.
Yiddish proverb

Employ words of compromise.
Every couple has differences of opinion. Words of compromise are necessary. Your goal is to resolve differences so both are satisfied. Some people fear apologizing will make them look weak and spineless. It takes character to genuinely apologize.

> "I never thought of it that way."
> "I can agree with you there."
> "I don't deserve a wife like you, but I've got arthritis and I don't deserve that either."

Thanks costs nothing.
Creole proverb

Words of appreciation.

Famous Kansas publisher George W. Crane wrote, "Appreciative words are the most powerful force for good on earth."

"Thank you."
"I have faith in you."
"You did a great job."
"I'm proud of you."
"I love you! I need you!"

*"Don't you understand? I love you! I need you!
I want to spend the rest of my vacation with you!"*

21   Ask for what you need.

This bugs me the most. That's when the husband thinks the wife knows where everything is, huh? Like they think the uterus is a tracking device. He comes in: "Hey Roseanne! Roseanne! Do we have any Cheetos left?" Like he can't go over and lift up the sofa cushion himself.

Roseanne Barr

If you have, give.
If you need, ask.

Malaysian proverb

Even couples with thriving marriages sometimes have trouble asking for what they need in their relationship. Why is it awkward to ask? Because we're afraid asking for what we want may lead to being rejected or to creating an uncomfortable situation.

"Now that the kids are grown and gone, I thought it might be a good time for us to have sex."

But, if you *don't* ask, it can become an unspoken and unresolved issue between you and your partner. So, go ahead and ask. Even if your asking creates a conflict, it's something you felt needed to be discussed and can now be talked about openly.

How to "ask for" what you need.

Mac, for me to be able to create I must have the right equipment, and I need a conducive writing environment.

I'm glad you're back to writing again, Fran. I think your poetry is incredible. I've got my college typewriter. I'll get it reconditioned for you.

How can I type on that old thing? I can't run a business, come home exhausted, be expected to fix dinner and then create. What's the matter with you?

Are you just looking for an excuse to avoid getting started?

What I'm looking for is a laptop computer, like yours. If you were a considerate husband you would get me one.

Honey, you're welcome to use my computer. Is there anything else keeping you from writing?

My desk lighting is all wrong.

That's easy to fix, I'll put in a blue-white fluorescent bulb.

I don't have any paper.

I have plenty of computer paper upstairs.

And, I have to go to the bathroom.

Uh huh.

You've never taught me to operate a computer. Those things give me a migraine headache. I'll end up having a stroke.

I should like to point out to you, sweetheart, that much great poetry and prose has been written with just a pen or pencil. We discussed everything you asked for, you're just plain stalling. Capiche?

Fuck off!

22   Compromise is not a dirty word.

Like it or not, the only solution to marital problems is to find a compromise. In a loving relationship it just doesn't work for either of you to get things all your way, even if you are convinced you are right. This approach would create such inequity and unfairness that the marriage would suffer.

John Gottman, *Why Marriages Succeed or Fail*

How to develop a compromise solution.
John Gottman recommends a seven-step approach to use in developing a satisfactory compromise solution.

1 Clearly identify the problem and hoped-for objective.
2 Recognize it is healthy to have different opinions.
3 Remember that no one has a monopoly on wisdom.
4 Conduct the discussion civilly: no insults or sobbing.
5 Give an open-minded hearing to all opinions.
6 Evaluate the pros and cons of the options.
7 Finalize a decision that is acceptable to both parties.

No one has a monopoly on wisdom.

Anonymous

I have learned that only two things are necessary to keep one's wife happy. First, let her think she's having her own way. Second, let her have it.

Lyndon B. Johnson

A compromise solution case study.

1 Identify the problem:

Should we sell our home in Baltimore county where we have lived for over 37 years?

2 Discuss different opinions:

I said, "I love living here. I don't want to move."
Fran replied, "One winter day, when you are away on a business trip, I will walk up to the mailbox and fall on the ice, freeze to death, and lie there until someone finds my cold body."

3 No one has a monopoly on wisdom:

We agreed no one had a monopoly on wisdom, but she thought I was being selfish and inconsiderate.

4 Conduct the discussion calmly and civilly:

"I'm lonely here!" she opined. "I hate it here. Do you hear me? I hate it here!"

5 Give a fair and open-minded hearing to all options:

"After I'm gone," Fran said, "and my dead remains are finally discovered in our driveway, the casserole brigade will come soon enough, and you'll be remarried before my frozen body has even thawed in the grave."

6 Evaluate the pros and cons.

"I can't live like this anymore!" she shrieked.

7 Finalize the mutually-arrived-at decision:

We *compromised* and sold the house.

IV Attitude

If you can't control what life brings you, you gotta control the attitude you bring to life

> *The greatest discovery of our generation is that human beings can alter their lives by altering their attitude of mind. As you think, so shall you be.*
>
> William James

The wedding night found Dan and Lorraine in a posh suite at the Hyatt, a bottle of champagne by the bed. Pulling a sexy negligee out of her suitcase, Lorraine was startled when Dan tossed her a pair of his pants and told her to put them on. They fell down in a pool around her knees.

"Honey, I can't wear your pants," she protested.

"Damn right, and don't you forget it," ordered the new husband. "I'm the man, and I wear the pants in the family."

Lorraine stepped out of her panties and tossed them to Dan. "Put these on, darling," she asked sweetly. Of course Dan couldn't pull the little scrap of cloth past his knees. "I can't get into your pants," he complained.

"That's right," she snapped, "and it's going to stay that way until you change your *attitude*!"

23   Laughter is the best medicine.

My darling wife was always glum,
I drowned her in a cask of rum.
And so made sure that she would stay,
In better spirits night and day.

Anonymous

Death is not the greatest loss in life. The greatest loss in life is what dies inside us when we live.
Norman Cousins

The eminent writer Norman Cousins was Editor of the *Saturday Review* for the better part of forty years. He was also the author of a dozen books and hundreds of essays and editorials. In the 1960s Cousins was stricken with a crippling, life-threatening collagen disease. He followed a regimen of high doses of vitamin C and of positive emotions, including daily doses of belly laughter with Marx Brothers movies and other humorous stimuli to make him laugh and heal. Cousins chronicled his recovery in the best-selling *Anatomy of an Illness.* In the book he affirmed that the "life force" may be the least understood force on earth.

Fran was active in World Federalists, a group dedicated to world peace. At the Maryland Chapter's 1985 annual event, Fran was dinner co-chairperson and Norman Cousins was the honoree.

I wasn't familiar with World Federalism, the *Saturday Review,* or Norman Cousins. Fran simply left a seating ticket for me at the registration desk. As I sat down at the table a well- dressed fellow joined me and said, "Hello, I'm Norman Cousins."

"Hi Norm," I replied. "I'm Mac, *what do you do?*"

He didn't appear eager to further our relationship.

What soap is to the body,
laughter is to the soul.
Yiddish proverb

Mr. Cousins told us that evening: "Every tomorrow has two choices—*anxiety* or *enthusiasm*. Upon your choice so will be your day—even your life. Your *attitude* can control your behavior."

Mr. Cousins concluded his remarks with a quote from Nicolas-Sebastien de Chamfort. "If taking vitamins doesn't keep you healthy enough, try more laughter; the most wasted of all days is one during which one has not laughed."

Life can be wildly tragic at times, and I've had my share. But whatever happens to you, in the final analysis you have got not to forget to laugh.
Katharine Hepburn

24   How to handle lust.

I've looked on a lot of women with lust. I've committed adultery in my heart many times. This is something that God recognizes I will do—and I have done it—and God forgives me for it.

Jimmy Carter
Interview in *Playboy* Magazine (1976)

To lust is to have a passionate or inordinate desire. When lust leads to extramarital infidelity, such behavior puts you at great financial, emotional and physical risk.

In a tree that you can't climb, there is always a thousand fruits.

Indian proverb

Jake was on his deathbed, with his wife Becky at his side. With tears streaming down his face, he said, "Becky, I must confess...." Becky interrupted, "Hush. Don't try to talk." But Jake insisted, "No, I want to die with a clean conscience. I must confess. I've lusted and been unfaithful to you." Becky replied, "Yes, I know. Why else would I have poisoned you?"

Our friend June is an accomplished artist. Some years ago she had a major showing of her works in Gallery 10 in Washington. As we walked through the exhibition rooms filled with June's large, abstract, awesome oil paintings, Fran and I became separated. An attractive young woman was looking at me intently. I figured it was my black eye patch and gave her my *Hathaway Man*-wounded-war-hero look.

To my surprise she approached me and said, "This is a little awkward for me to say, but I couldn't help staring at you tonight. May ask you something personal?"

I looked around the gallery and saw no sight of Fran. I gazed at this attractive young woman and thought, "My business is in the toilet, my eye operation was unsuccessful, this black eye patch must make me look sexy. Maybe my luck is changing."

Looking deeply into her limpid blue eyes, I whispered: "Certainly, my dear, you may speak freely."

"I couldn't help noticing the large separation between your two front teeth," she said. "My little boy has the same problem. I'm concerned, do you think he should have braces?"

> *He who has separation in teeth and lusts for Venus, may end up like John Wayne Bobbitt with separation of his marriage and also of his penis.*

25 Open a relationship bank account.

The best proof
of love is trust.
Dr. Joyce Brothers

A "Relationship Bank Account" is a metaphor to describe the love and trust that accrue in a healthy relationship.

Acts of friendship, respect, loyalty, and dependability are *deposits* into the account.

When one feels upset, angry and unappreciated, there is a tendency to *withdraw*, both metaphorically and physically.

When the Relationship Bank Account is in the black, with a reservoir of good will, then minor disagreements will remain just that—*minor.*

"And do you, Gwen, trust this man no
further than you can throw him?"

In the mid-1970s Fran was writing poetry. She was published in a volume of poetry entitled *Rye Bread: Women Poets Rising.* On one occasion, Fran asked if I minded if she went off for a winter poetry weekend.

"What's a poetry weekend?"

"Well, a group from Towson State are going to Ocean City to write and critique poetry and stuff like that."

Upon her return Sunday night, Fran seemed euphoric.

"The group," she said, "walked in the snow, sat by the fire, held hands, drank cheap wine, read poetry, wrote poetry, and everyone had an incredible experience."

"Did you find time for writing?" I asked sarcastically. Fran showed me a poem she had written.

Trust is like an icicle—
if once it melts, that's
the end of it.
Anonymous

> *You are the sea*
> *you covet me*
> *Your tide washes away*
> *my loneliness*
> *Without you I am a shell*
> *drifting weightless*
> *in a North wind.*

"Wow," I said, "what a terrific poem, and it testifies to our trusting and loving relationship. Your words are sensitive and meaningful. And to think, you wrote this especially for me. It is me that's coveting you and washing away your loneliness, isn't it? Fran? FRAN?"

26 Loyalty—love's beachhead on the shores of eternity.

The sum which two married people owe to one another defies calculation. It is an infinite debt, which can only be discharged through all eternity.

Johann Wolfgang von Goethe
Elective Affinities (1808),bk. I, ch.9

Loyalty is love's beachhead on the shores of eternity.
Dr. Jose Albornoz is a Colombian-born psychiatrist and a dear friend. On his 35th wedding anniversary, he dedicated the following poem to his wife, Betty.

*Let this be words from the deeper depth of my heart
to say to you all here
look at her
she is my precious
she is my caretaker*

*She has given me all these beautiful children
and their children*

*And she has been loyal to me beyond description
and beyond reason*

*We celebrate today not that we have been together
for thirty-five years*

*We celebrate that we are together tonight
in honor and good health*

We celebrate that I can write one more poem to her
because she is a living monument
to what every wife should be

Because she is full of love and her love has
built for us a beachhead on the shores of eternity

Dr. Jose M. Albornoz (1992).

Loyalty means not airing differences in public.
Loyalty means you show respect to your spouse, particularly
in public, and you don't correct him/her or make your
partner the object of jokes. When we lived in Baltimore
County, we were given a Siamese cat named Cleopatra. She
was a graceful and beautiful animal and required little
looking after. We had no kitty litter box. I presumed that
whenever she had to go, one of the boys or Fran would
just open the door and let Cleopatra out.

Some weeks after her arrival on the scene, I noticed
our small bedroom had a funny odor. I thought Fran was
having a little gastrointestinal problem and decided not to
comment.

After a few days elapsed, Fran eyed me strangely and
said, "What is that awful smell?" She got down on her
knees, looked under the bed, and in the muslin lining
found *evidence*.

The next morning, as our sons Jamie, Scott, and Adam,
and I were eating breakfast, Fran pointed to the cat, glared,
and announced, "That cat goes or I go!"

Before we had a chance to discuss the option or vote
or anything, Cleopatra began to spin in a circle and
collapsed. The vet reported she died of a hemorrhaging
brain tumor.

Differences between
husband and wife
should not be aired
in the marketplace.
African proverb

The last time I told this story, Fran took me aside and said, "When you tell that cat story—with the cute bit about a gastrointestinal problem, it's offensive and insulting to me, and I would appreciate it if you would stop repeating it in public."

I thought about what she said and agreed I wasn't exemplifying *loyalty* by telling it. I also remembered Fran glaring at the cat, pointing her finger, and the cat suddenly *dropping dead*.

27 Commitment is more than participation.

Commitment is what transforms a promise into reality.
Abraham Lincoln

The acorn becomes an oak by means of automatic growth; no commitment is necessary. The kitten similarly becomes a cat on the basis of instinct. Nature and being are identical in creatures like them. But a man or woman becomes fully human only by his or her choices and his or her commitment to them. People attain worth and dignity by the multitude of decisions they make from day by day. These decisions require courage.
Rollo May, *The Courage to Create*, (1994)

"And do you, Rebecca, promise to make love only to Richard, month after month, year after year, and decade after decade, until one of you is dead?"

The premise of any long term relationship is the mutual understanding that each partner can be counted on to keep commitments and promises. Without commitment, people feel more insecure and are likely to withhold things that are bothering them—withholding erodes closeness.

Commitment vs Participation.

Marriage means commitment.
Of course, so does insanity.
Anonymous

The chicken and the pig were discussing the matter. The chicken said proudly, "I give eggs every single morning—I'm committed."

"Giving eggs isn't commitment, it's participation," said the pig. "Giving ham is a commitment."

28   Things do not change—we change.

He who hath so little knowledge of human nature as to seek happiness by changing anything but his own disposition, will waste his life in fruitless efforts and multiply the grief he proposes to remove.

Samuel Johnson

Before you prepare to improve the world, look around your own house three times.

Chinese proverb

Accept change and support growth in yourself and your mate.

You hear the phrase "marry and settle down," which implies life becomes serene and peaceful after marriage. Unfortunately, this is far from the truth. Married life is normally one long series of experiments in accommodation. Before marriage, the liaison is characterized by sharing mutually agreeable and pleasurable activities. After marriage, you take life as it comes. The relationship now involves responsibilities that may cause stress and require adjustment and change.

Changing our own attitudes and behavior may be daunting, but trying to effect change in others is far more difficult. As Tolstoy said, "Everybody thinks of changing humanity, but nobody thinks of changing themselves."

"I'm not asking you to change your spots. I'm just asking you to take out the garbage."

Handling change.

EXAMPLE: How to handle a request for change.

"Work, work, work!" Fran griped. "Can't you ever talk to me. I might as well be talking to the moon. I didn't get married to watch N.Y.P.D. reruns the rest of my life!" I calmly listened to her critical comment and resisted responding in kind. I thought, "What is behind this outburst? Fran must be feeling lonely. She is in need of companionship."

"Honey," I said, "I should plan more fun things for us to do together. I promise I will change and be the kind of husband you deserve. I will surprise you with romantic and exciting activities. I will create magic moments just for the two of us. Would you like that, sweetheart?"

"Be quiet!" she hissed, "I'm watching the episode where Jimmy Smits is dying."

Life is constant readjustment to our surroundings.

I respect my mother-in-law, Bess. She was in her mid-eighties when we urged her to give up driving.

Bess resisted, saying, "I drive just fine, thank you. Everywhere I go people *wave* to me." She demonstrated the greetings she had been receiving by extending the middle index finger of her right hand up in the air.

Bess stopped driving and also agreed, reluctantly, to sell her home and the garden she loved, to move into an assisted-care, retirement environment. It was a necessary but difficult adjustment, but she kept her sense of humor and feistiness.

It's hard for me to get used to these changing times. I can remember when the air was clean, and sex was dirty.
George Burns

On one visit, we found the Serenity Prayer by
Reinhold Neibuhr Scotch-taped to her refrigerator. Bess
isn't an alcoholic—she's a milk-oholic—but when you boil
down accepting *change*, it's embodied in the profound
words on Bess's refrigerator.

> *God grant me the serenity to accept the things I*
> *cannot change; courage to change the things I can;*
> *And wisdom to know the difference.*

All I can do is play the game
the way the cards fall.
James Michener

29 Sharing is unconditional giving.

Sharing is an essential part of a relationship. If you cannot share you cannot give. If you cannot give, you cannot love. Sharing is unconditional giving. If you share but expect something in return you are not sharing, you are trading.

Howard J. Rankin, *10 Steps to a Great Relationship*

Sharing joy is double joy; sharing sorrow is half sorrow.

Swedish proverb

We were invited to attend a church service by Preston, a close friend who was being installed as president of the ushers. The congregation was African-American. We were the only white people present. Since the occasion was the installation of new officers, the church had arranged for two gospel groups to participate. The minister preached a meaningful sermon; the assembly swayed to organ music; the gospel singers sang; the ushers, dressed in tuxedos—led by Preston—strutted down the aisle in a rhythmic cadence.

The service concluded with the minister asking if either Fran or I, as Preston's guests, would care to say anything. I rose self-consciously and thanked everyone for the privilege of attending. As I sat down, Fran rose to her feet, looking over the gathering, who were all turning around in their seats to look at *us*. She began to clap her hands and sing.

"HE'S GOT THE WHOLE WIDE WO—RLD IN HIS HANDS."

The congregation gaped in wide-eyed amazement. I was in shock. Fran continued singing, and one gospel group picked up the beat and joined in. Then, the second gospel group added their voices, followed by the organist and the parishioners.

Everyone held hands and sang—the church rocked with *"He's got the whole wide world in his hands."*

Fran was singing, and I was eyeing the exits— questioning her sanity. When the song and the service ended, the applause was deafening. People rushed over, pinned on a corsage, kissed and hugged my wife.

In that church on that Sunday, Fran risked potential embarrassment to present *her* offering—of music.

Sharing is unconditional giving.

True happiness lies in giving it to others.
Indian proverb

30   Let there be spaces in your togetherness.

*You were born together, and together you
shall be forevermore,
    But let there be spaces in your togetherness,
And stand together yet not too near together:
    For the pillars of the temple stand apart.
And the oak tree and the cypress grow
    not in each other's shadow.*

Kahlil Gibran
The Prophet (1923). On Marriage

Most of us desire a certain amount of personal space, and married partners are no exception. According to a Hindu proverb, "You grow only when you are alone."

We need time to be alone or with friends— time to pursue individual interests. A healthy relationship is when partners not only have fulfilling lives and identities outside the relationship, but *actively* encourage each other to do so.

"Gotta run, sweetheart. By the way, that was one fabulous job you did raising the children."

I love golf. When our boys were young, I couldn't play as often as I would have liked. I discussed the situation with my wife.

"Honey, I really *need some space.* I want to play golf more often. Golf is healthy, outdoor exercise, and if I don't play two or three times a week I will lose 'muscle memory.' Then I might just as well give up the game. I'd be miserable. You wouldn't want me to do that, would you, Fran dear?"

"I've had it up to here with your golf," she said.

"I didn't sacrifice my career to be your slave, taking care of the house and the children, while you travel around the country on so-called business trips. Then you come home and want to spend the weekends on the golf course. Why can't you spend time with me? I think you're selfish and inconsiderate. You would rather play golf with your buddies than be with me. Are you gay?"

"Fran, Kahlil Gibran's words have been translated into more than twenty languages. He was considered by Arabic-speaking people the genius of his age. He expressed the deepest impulses of man's heart and soul. In *The Prophet*, which was his greatest achievement, Gibran said, 'The oak tree and the cypress grow not in each other's shadow.' He meant that it's good to be together but not too close together."

" So...BIG DEAL, that's *his* opinion."

A palm tree growing in the shade will not bear ripe fruit.

Afghanistan proverb

31   Respect is love in plain clothes.

If you don't respect the other person,
you're gonna have a lot of trouble.
Morrie Schwartz
Mitch Albom, *Tuesdays with Morrie*

Treat your partner as the unique individual he/she really is. In the 1960s Fran was very active in local theater. A prospective customer from Chicago was coming to Baltimore to inspect our company's manufacturing facilities. I entertained him at one of the city's best restaurants, the Chesapeake. Fran joined us for dinner. My business prospect, Howard, asked my wife about her career. Fran explained she had recently finished playing a leading role of Lalume in *Kismet*, and she and some other actors from the *Kismet* cast were hired to perform character roles in a film that was being shot that very evening.

Since Howard seemed interested, Fran invited us to go along and watch the filming. We drove to an eerie-looking building on St. Paul Street, parked and walked up three flights.

When Fran knocked on the door, a young man opened it part-way and asked, "Who are you?"

Fran gave her name and the guy said, "Are you one of the prostitutes?"

Fran answered, "Yes, I believe so."

"Who are those two?" he asked, pointing to us.

"They are just here to watch," Fran replied.

We all went into the apartment. Howard and I huddled in a corner while the cast assembled. The actresses put on

Trying to build a marriage without respect is like trying to build a home on quicksand.
African proverb

togas (nightgowns), and the filming began. I'm told that the movie's subject was religious, *Lazarus Reborn*, or something like that. The film was being produced by a Johns Hopkins University graduate student as his thesis, or maybe just a great way to pick up women. As he was leaving town, Howard said, "This has been the most exciting visit I've ever made to a supplier." He added, "Your wife, Fran, is a very unique individual; I admire the way you respect her career interests."

"You can say that again, Howard!"

"Your mom's a very special person."

#32   Treasure your children.

*I asked professors who teach the meaning of life to tell me
what happiness is.
And I went to famous executives who boss the work of
thousands of men.
They all shook their heads and gave me a smile as though
I was trying to fool with them.
And then one Sunday afternoon I wandered out along the
Desplaines river.
And I saw a crowd of Hungarians under the trees with their
women and children and a keg of beer and an accordion.*
Happiness from *Chicago Poems* by Carl Sandburg

*Govern a family as
you would cook a
small fish—very gently.*
Chinese proverb

Fran and I have been blessed with three decent, caring, and loving sons: Jamie, Scott, and Adam. As our children grew into adulthood, it wasn't easy to cut the cord and let go.

"I've had a rough day, honey. Tell me everybody's name again."

You are the bow...
let them go.

> *You are the bows from which your children are sent forth. Let your bending be for gladness, for even as he loves the arrow that flies, so he loves the bow that is stable.*
>
> Kahlil Gibran
> *The Prophet* (1923). On Marriage

Jamie the surfer.

> *Rough seas, surfer man*
> *white foam on the horizon*
> *swells, like too many suds*
> *in the washing machine*
>
> *I watched you leap into the sea,*
> *surfer man*
> *your tight body charged*
> *against the incoming tide.*
>
> *Turning at the right moment*
> *to ride the curling wave*
> *into shore, then out again.*
>
> *Defy the shark's fin,*
> *leap with the Dolphin,*
> *feel the warmth of the August Sea.*
> *Be, Be*
> *And I will understand.*
>
> Fran Mahr

Jamie, the eldest, *went forth* on a surfboard. He loved to surf and traveled the East Coast, California, Central America, and Hawaii to ride the big waves.

Children have more need of models than critics.

French proverb

As concerned parents, while Jamie was in college in 1974, we voiced our uneasiness about his hanging out with long-haired surfers who practiced Transcendental Meditation and gave the impression life was a series of endless summers.

He told us, "There's a lot of drugs and alcohol used on our college campus. At the Billy Joel concert last week, kids were carried out on stretchers from overdosing. Surfers don't need the dope or booze. We get a high off of the surfing, plus it's great exercise. Not to worry."

While in college, Jamie paid for his surfing trips by painting houses. Prior to a Costa Rican trip, he was a little short of cash. He asked his grandmother, Bess, if he could paint her house exterior.

As he was finishing the job—the day before departure —it rained. The paint was water-based white. Our son completed the job in the rain, collected his money, and left for Costa Rica.

His grandmother's house had an interesting off-white streaky patina, like an early Jackson Pollock painting.

Unfortunately, when the house was eventually sold, the new buyers evidenced little appreciation for modern art.

Today, Jamie is national sales manager for Berwick Ribbon, the world's largest ribbon and bow manufacturer. He lives in Dallas with his wife, Sherry, and two children, Maureen and Harry. Jamie may be a little too old to ride a surfboard, but still finds excitement being in the water—fishing for salmon in Alaska.

Scott the artist. Scott, the middle son, was the talented rebel. At four years old, he got annoyed with us, said, "I'm running away!" took some clothes and left the house. Fran became concerned and had me check Scott's whereabouts.

I saw him sitting on the street curb in front of our house. When I asked what he was doing there, Scott replied, "I'm not allowed to cross the street by myself."

Scott has a kind and generous spirit. When he first learned to drive, he accidentally bumped into the rear of a car driven by an elderly couple. They got out looked at the minor dent and said, "It's nothing to worry about, son."

"Accidents like this can cause serious whiplash," Scott advised them. "You should immediately go to Sinai Hospital and have it checked out." They agreed to do so, and thanked him.

That evening Scott related the story to us. While we appreciated his loving, caring nature, we held our breath waiting for a call from some personal injury lawyer. He hasn't called yet. I think the statute of limitations ran out twenty-five years ago.

Once Scott *was* able to cross the street alone, there was no stopping him. As an award-winning graphic designer, his interests led him to many parts of the world, including working several years in Bangkok, Thailand and teaching at the Parsons School of Design in New York City.

Several years ago, just before 9:00 a.m., Scott was having coffee with a neighbor on the roof of his apartment building located in New York's East Village. As he looked over the Manhattan skyline he was shocked to see a smoking hole in the north tower of the World Trade Center, a few blocks away.

He heard the sound of an overhead plane, and at 9:03 a.m., Scott saw United Airlines Flight 175 from Boston crash into the south tower and explode. Both buildings were burning.

Neighbors and people in adjoining buildings appeared on their rooftops screaming and pointing.

Scott rushed down to his apartment, turned on the TV to catch the news and heard that at 9:43 a.m. American Airlines Flight 77 had also crashed into the Pentagon.

Returning to the unimaginable scene from the roof, at 10:05, he witnessed in horror the south tower of the World Trade Center collapse, plummeting into the street with massive clouds of dust and debris forming and slowly drifting away from the building.

Twenty-three minutes later, the north tower collapsed from the top down as if it were peeled apart, releasing another tremendous cloud of smoke.

At 11:02, New York City Mayor Rudolph Giuliani ordered the evacuation of the area south of Canal Street. With all transportation shut down, Scott observed throngs of people covered in dirt and filth struggling away from the World Trade Center, scrambling for telephones to call loved ones. The air smelled acrid and foul.

For Scott, the horrific experience was traumatizing. He left New York to visit with a dear friend, Karen, who lived in Virginia. Upon arriving at Karen's lovely apartment in Alexandria, he looked out the window only to discover the view faced directly toward the mangled section of the Pentagon that had collapsed under the impact of the hijacker's plane crash.

Words are but dwarfs,
examples are giants.
Luxembourg proverb

Returning to New York, Scott experienced frequent orange alerts, building evacuations, and was upset by hearing overhead aircraft. His best friend, Michael, called from Germany and invited him to get away from the tragedy for a brief respite.

Scott flew to Hamburg, Germany to calm down. A few days later the Euro was introduced into Germany, and Scott went to a nearby branch of Deutche Bank to exchange travelers checks. As he was waiting in line, three armed men entered the bank. One grabbed a young woman, putting a hand over her mouth and a serrated-edged hunting knife to her throat. The tellers fearfully advised the men that the money was in a time-lock safe that couldn't be opened. The robbers lined up the fifteen customers, taking their watches and money.

Scott left the chaos of New York City only to become a hostage in a bank robbery in Germany.

Adam the retailer. Adam, our youngest son, left Baltimore at five years old to attend his first Presidential news conference. Adam wore his gray flannel suit, with short pants and striped bow tie, to go the White House. He took some chewing gum Fran had given him. Adam was invited and accompanied by our friend and White House correspondent, Muriel Dobbin, who filed this story:

Every future is not far away.
German proverb

> "On the south lawn of the White House today three red-and-white striped tents were erected and gallons of pink lemonade and piles of cookies were laid in.
>
> Five-year-old Adam Mahr sat sedately in his chair for at least four minutes before discarding his jacket, asking whether the President was going to dance and announcing that he was hungry.

The most important thing that parents can teach their children is how to get along without them.

Frank A. Clark

He was one of more than 600 children invited to attend President Johnson's first "kiddie-conference," to which family and friends of reporters were invited. While the president discussed the economy, Adam made bubbling sounds.

After the press conference, everybody headed for the lemonade bowls, including President Johnson and Adam. They met over a paper cup of tart pink liquid, and Adam, whose head was not as high as the President's waist, shook the Presidential hand and asked him for some more cookies.

Adam suddenly remembered the gum in his jacket pocket. He tugged gently at the President's coat, but the tall man was shaking the hand of a child two people away. Adam was disappointed until he looked at the flattened package of gum that he had been offering.

It was empty.

Muriel Dobbin, *Baltimore Sun,* May 6, 1964

Adam started his retail career at the age of fourteen, working part- time for a drugstore in Ocean City, Maryland. At sixteen he managed a clothing store, and after college entered a Lord and Taylor Department Store training program in New York.

Now, Adam owns two retail stores called A Mano; one in Georgetown, and the other in Naples, Florida.

The *Washington Post* said, "A Mano is a bright spot on the Washington shopping scene. Baltimore native Adam Mahr goes to Europe six times a year, finds designs he likes, and works with the artisans in the pottery factories to produce the French and Italian pottery for his charming shop."

Good parents give their children Roots and Wings: Roots to know where home is, wings to fly away and exercise what's been taught them.

Jonas Salk

33 Honor your in-laws.

Whoever buys a house must examine the beams; whoever wants a wife must look at the mother.
Chinese proverb

As soon as the newlyweds returned from their honeymoon, the young bride called her mother.

"How did everything go?" her mother asked.

"Oh Mother," she began, "The honeymoon was wonderful! So romantic, we had a terrific time. But Mother, on the way back, Albert started using really horrible language. Stuff I'd never heard before, really terrible four-letter words. Come and get me and take me home. Please, Mother!" the new bride sobbed over the phone.

"Honey," the mother countered, "what four-letter words?"

"I can't tell you, Mother, they are too awful! Come and get me right away, please!"

"My God, it's your mother!"

"Darling, you must tell me what has gotten you so upset....Tell Mother what four-letter words he used."

Still sobbing, the bride said, "Mother, words like *dust, wash, iron, cook.*"

I love my mother-in-law, Bess. She is an independent and feisty lady. Bess is fiercely proud of her family. A few years ago her Annapolis, Maryland, High School graduating class had their 70th reunion. Everyone was supposed to bring something to say or read.

The night before the reunion Bess called Fran in a panic because she had nothing to read. I remembered an old Irish poem that might be *perfect* for the occasion, but had forgotten the words.

Fran said, "Call Mike, the owner of the Claddagh Pub, on O'Donnell Street, he'll know. It's an Irish pub."

At 8 P.M. I called Mike. He yelled down the bar, "Hey, you guys, hold it down a minute. Who knows the words to 'when the road comes to greet you'?" I heard people in the bar hooting and laughing. Mike came back with the words.

> *May the road rise to meet you*
> *May the wind always be at your back*
> *May the sun shine warm upon your face*
> *The rain fall soft upon your fields*
> *And until we meet again*
> *May God hold you in the palm of his hand.*

We called Bess and gave her the poem. During the next day's luncheon Bess recited her offering. Everyone applauded and asked where she had found such a touching and meaningful poem. Bess responded proudly, "My daughter Frances wrote it!"

*What cannot be cured
must be endured.*
Bess Schleider

In 1979 Fran started a business, The Paper Warehouse. It was a retail store featuring discount gift wrappings and party goods. "A Penny Pincher's Paradise," Fran used to call it.

The discount party goods store concept was new in 1979, and the business was successful. It was named "Best in Baltimore" by *Baltimore Magazine* for "Party Goods" category. Eventually The Paper Warehouse expanded to a four-store chain.

Fran's friends and family assisted in various ways. Her mother, Bess, wanted to help, so Fran had her print the store's name—with a black magic marker—on plain yellow shopping bags. These bags were used by customers to carry out their purchases. Bess made a slight error; instead of writing *The Paper Warehouse*, she printed THE PAPER WHOREHOUSE on the bags. Store traffic picked up the following week. (It pays to advertise.)

My mother-in-law, Bess, as of this writing, is 93 years old. She's not doing too well, with a myriad of serious ailments. Bess is testy and speaks her mind. Someone said to her on her 90th birthday, "Why do you use a cane, Bess?"

She snapped, "Just in case anyone tries to rape me, I'll hit him on the—you know what." Then added, "The good Lord watches over old fools and damn fools. He watches me real good."

At the end of one visit with Bess at the nursing home, I kissed her on the forehead, and she said, "I love you and your whole *damn* family." That's my mother-in-law.

34   Learn to cope with stress.

There are three specific ways that stress has a negative effect on marriage. It saps us of the strength we need to renew our love. It turns us from allies into adversaries, as we blame each other. And stress makes us hostile competitors for each other's sympathy.

Marriage Partnership magazine

BOOTH

Rule #1: Don't sweat the small stuff. Rule #2: It's almost all small stuff.

Robert S. Elliot

"I want you to take some time off! Relax a little."

Here are five guidelines for dealing with stress that were taught to congressional aides by psychologists at a stress management seminar hosted by the American Psychological Association.

1 **Exercise**: During lunch hour or at the end of the workday. Even a twenty-minute walk a day can relieve stress.

2 **Breathe deeply for relaxation**: Close your eyes and take slow deep breaths. Feel your muscles loosen and let go. It takes less than a minute.

3 **Maintain a positive attitude**: Change how you think, and you can change how you feel.

4 **Delay action until your emotion subsides**: Build in a delay, so that if you decide to take action, it'll be well thought out.

5 **Find supportive friends**: Friends can be good medicine. Talking to supportive colleagues can help you let off steam, clarify feelings, and collect your thoughts.

Attend a stress management clinic.

"I spent two hundred dollars," my wife announced, "and signed us both up for a stress clinic at the Holiday Inn."

"That's ridiculous!" I replied. "I handle tons of stress at work. Besides, I can't waste a whole day sitting around with a bunch of neurotics. I'm not going—and that's final."

As we entered the Holiday Inn, we met our instructor, a doctor of internal medicine, who explained that recent medical findings prove stress is a killer!

"How many of you could drink a fifth of vodka in one sitting?" he asked. The class tittered. "You could if you were an alcoholic," he continued, "though it's destructive to your kidneys and liver.

Living in worry invites death in a hurry.
American proverb

"How many of you are business executives who work with stressful situations all day—though the stress might be destructive to your heart?" He had my attention. The instructor spoke of the importance of exercise and meditation. "Current research on meditation," he added, "supports claims that the practice of this ancient discipline can tap into our unconscious minds and provide a technique for relaxation."

Fran and I remained at the Holiday Inn to eat during the lunch break, because it was raining hard outside.

At lunch she said, "Now aren't you happy I signed us up for this clinic?"

"Yes, but frankly, dear, you're so excitable, you need this stress training much more than I do."

"How dare you say that to me!" she fumed. "I was the one who made this happen, who brought you here, who treated you to the course. I'm going home."

I chased after her through the pouring rain to the car.

"Take me home," she yelled, "Right now!"

"Fran, this is ridiculous, we're in a stress management course, and here we are fighting during intermission."

"Take me home or I swear I'll call a cab," she sputtered.

The rain was pouring off both of us. I spoke those marvelous, healing words: "Fran, I'm sorry I upset you. Will you please forgive me?"

Either those magical words worked, or Fran didn't want to waste the two hundred dollars she had invested in the course. Soaking wet, we returned for the afternoon session to further enhance our loving relationship and our proficiency in coping with stress.

Bad is never good,
until worse happens.
Danish proverb

35   Meditation can quiet your mind and relax your body.

Truth is perfect and complete in itself. Zen is simply the expression of truth. In Zen meditation, you are the mirror reflecting the solution of your problems.

Zen Master Dogen

Zen question:
If a man is in the forest talking to himself, with no women present, is he still wrong?

Millions of people practice Zen meditation and obtain its fruits. You can learn the basics of meditation in a few minutes. Don't doubt its possibilities because of the simplicity of the method.

After our stress clinic, I started meditating daily and benefited from the experience. I didn't proselytize. If friends were aware of what I was doing and asked me to show them my approach, I was happy to help. There is no one right way to meditate. Whichever meditation technique enables you to breathe deeply, develop an inner calmness, and works for *you*—works!

A friend was going through a stressful period. His wife asked if I would teach him meditation. The next day he joined in my five-step meditation routine. I cautioned it takes time, practice and patience to enjoy the *full* benefits of the experience.

A week later, the phone rang. "My husband's in the bedroom meditating," his wife said, "but he's stuck on step three, and he's forgotten step four. Quick, tell me what he's supposed to do next—he's hyperventilating."

Try this meditation yourself—it's easy!

Here's my favorite meditation exercise. Allow 30 minutes.

When you can't find peace within yourself, it's useless to seek it elsewhere.
French proverb

1 Find a spot to sit quietly, comfortably and undisturbed.

Sit upright with your hands in your lap, back straight, eyes closed, nose pointing at your navel.

2 Concentrate on your breathing.

For fifteen minutes, breathe deeply and exhale slowly. Breathe through your nose. Let your breath find a natural rhythm, and your body relax. Keep your mind a blank and clear of any thoughts. Many thoughts will crowd into your head; ignore them, let them go. It takes a little practice, be patient. Feel as though your breath enters through the top of your head and washes down to your toes.

3 Tense your muscles.

For five minutes: Starting with your toes, tense tightly for a count of twenty. Relax and take two very slow deep breaths. Tighten your legs, your buttocks, your abdomen, then your shoulders and neck muscles. After each muscle group is tensed for a count of twenty, relax

"It was a very bleak period in my life, Louie. Martinis didn't help. Religion didn't help. Psychiatry didn't help. Transcendental meditation didn't help. Yoga didn't help. But Martinis helped a little."

and breathe deeply again. Next, clench your fists and then your forearms. Finally, with eyes still closed, tense all the muscle groups at one time, always breathing normally during the muscle tightening, and breathing deeply between tensing exercises.

4 Peaceful place.
For five minutes, focus on a place in nature you remember as being peaceful and beautiful: A quiet beach, a Zen rock garden, a sunset, a park, or a place in your imagination. See it in your mind's eye. The colors, the scenery, the sounds or the lack of sounds. Revisit, relax and enjoy this special place and let yourself feel peaceful.

5 Problem solving (optional).
You have now spent twenty-five minutes oxygenating your brain, tensing your muscles, relaxing and feeling peaceful. Your mind is now the *clearest* it will be all day. Ask yourself, "What's my biggest burden?" It usually sits there in the forefront of your conscious mind.

Take the last five minutes to think about how it can be resolved. There is no magic solution to life's problems. You will soon realize that your problems are manageable and you're gaining an intuitive power hitherto unnoticed.

My son has taken up meditation. At least it's better than sitting around and doing nothing.
Max Kaufman

36   Stay healthy and physically fit.

A vigorous five-mile walk will do more good for an unhappy but otherwise healthy adult than all the medicine and psychology in the world.

Dr. Paul Dudley White

By exercising vigorously at least three times a week and eating a healthy diet, you will be better able to manage stress, sleep better, feel healthier and enjoy life more. Aerobic exercises strengthen the heart and oxygenate the blood. The word "aerobic" literally means "with oxygen." Bike riding, swimming, jogging, handball, tennis, basketball — all are aerobic exercises.

My favorite aerobic exercise is swimming. In my fifties, I went to the downtown YMCA to swim laps.

One Sunday, Fran was reading a newspaper article featuring one of the nation's top landscape architects.

"Why don't we build a pool?" she inquired. "It would be great aerobic exercise and it would save money, because we wouldn't rent an apartment in Ocean City anymore."

"Uh huh," I said.

Fran continued, "I wonder if this landscape person would design one for us?"

"Sure," I replied facetiously, "I know he would jump at the chance to come to Baltimore to design a cheap swimming pool." I heard Fran speaking on the phone.

"May I call you Jim? I *do* understand you have to be in Tokyo on Wednesday, Jim, but couldn't you pleeeese come to Baltimore tomorrow?"

The only way to keep your health is to eat what you don't want, drink what you don't like, and do what you'd rather not.

Mark Twain

He who has health has hope, and he who has hope has everything.

Arabian proverb

I smiled at the absurdity of a nationally acclaimed landscape designer dropping everything and coming to see Fran. Then I heard her say, "Thank you, Jim, I'll meet you at the train."

"What the hell are you doing?" I yelled. "We can't afford anyone like that."

"Well, it doesn't hurt to ask, does it?" she responded.

The next day Fran called me at my office and said, "Come home quick, Jim has created a plan for *the Mahr Pond.*"

"Pond...what pond?"

When I arrived, the father of American landscape design described his vision. "The silent rhythms and patterns of Mahr Pond will remind you of one of the most famous temple gardens in Japan, that of Ryoan-ji, in Kyoto. The stream at the end of your property will be diverted and pumped up to cascade in a waterfall over the rocks—into a naturally wooded *pond.* The pond garden itself will be made of small stones resting on a bed of off-white gravel. A few large boulders will be positioned with great simplicity—expressing our understanding of Zen enlightenment..."

"May I call you Jim?" I interrupted. "I have a few questions: First, I am very interested in lap swimming for aerobic exercise. Will I be able to do that in this pool...er, pond plan?"

"No," he answered.

"Next, I like to swim in the morning. This pool seems to be located at the far end of the property. Isn't that inconvenient?"

"Yes," Jim said. "But in this location everything, even a blade of grass, will express ultimate reality. Thus it can be said the Mahr Pond and Garden of itself suggests to us absolute value."

"Aren't there lots of bugs and insects out in the woods where you propose the Mahr whatever would be located—especially at night with lighting?"

"Yes," he said. "At night you will see the garden and pool framed by the trees as we sense the truth of the forest stretching out boundlessly."

"How much will this thing cost?"

"Now Mac," Fran said, "we're just in the concept stage."

"Well, Jim, just how much conceptually do you think the pool will cost?"

A number was mentioned, a very large number.

"You expect me to pay that amount for a pond that I can't swim laps in; that's a long distance from the house, and one where I'll get eaten up alive by bugs?"

"You can still swim your laps at the Y," Fran piped in.

Jim turned out to be an OK guy. For a reasonable fee he created a *pool* landscape design, and we hired a local contractor to implement the plan. The Mahr Pool wasn't featured in *House and Garden* Magazine. It was a plastic, in-ground, Buster Crabbe pool, but I *could* swim laps in it, the pool *was* near the house *and* as for the proposed economic savings, Fran was right, we *did* stop *renting* an apartment in Ocean City. Instead, we bought one.

V

Renewal

If you want to *renew* your marriage, life will provide the canvas, you gotta do the painting

I like you
        after all these years
I still like you
This feeling
        it seems to grow
like the gray
        creeping round
        your ears.
                Fran Mahr

Happiness itself does not stay, only moments of happiness do.
        Russian proverb

In the bride-and-groom days, you had more time for shared fun and recreation. As years go by, with the normal day-to-day stresses of work and family, it becomes increasingly difficult to schedule renewal time—for vacations and romantic experiences.

Here are seven *renewal* ideas to treat yourself to:

1 Watch more sunsets.
2 Share romantic moments.
3 Take a weekend mini-vacation.
4 Give a gift for no reason.
5 Be spontaneous.
6 Plan a party.
7 Travel to interesting places.

37   Watch more sunsets.

If I had my life to live over, I would take more trips, pick more daisies, climb more mountains, swim more rivers, and watch more sunsets. I've had my moments, and if I had it to do over again, I'd try to have nothing else, just moments, one after the other.

Nadine Stair (at age 89)

There is something romantic about sharing a beautiful sunset. We went to the Grand Canyon to see the spectacular vista—to Indian Point—the best location to view the sun going down over the canyon looking west across the mountains.

Fran eyed children climbing on the railings constructed to prevent anyone's falling five thousand feet to the canyon floor. Even though parents hovered nearby, Fran catastrophized. She felt this was a "disaster waiting to happen," and refused to hang around and watch. We left before the romantic sunset.

During the night I felt a *rumbling* in our hotel room. Fran awoke and said, "What's that shaking?"

"It's just the plumbing," I told her.

Twenty minutes later, we were startled with a jolt. I called the desk and asked, "Is there any problem I should know about?"

"We had an earthquake tremor," the clerk replied.

"Have you ever had an earthquake tremor before?" I asked.

"Last year," she said, "but we had no death or devastation."

The secret of health for both mind and body, is to live the present moment wisely and earnestly.

Buddha

"No death or devastation?" I repeated aloud.

Hearing those words, Fran arose from her bed, gathered the suitcases, and began hurling stuff in. As she rushed out the door, she screamed, "I'm going to Alburquerque. You can come with me...or stay here and die!"

Someday I would like to go to the Grand Canyon and see the sunset from Indian Point. I understand that when you've seen that, you've seen EVERYTHING.

"Well, now we've seen it."

38 Share romantic moments.

Although it is possible to share a romantic moment almost anywhere, location and setting are important in creating the right atmosphere and associations. The things NOT to take with you on a romantic interlude are: children; in-laws; laptops; pets; or work. Romance is, above all, about making your partner feel special, and you can only do that by paying him or her some attention.

Howard J. Rankin, *10 Steps to a Great Relationship*

Reserve the bridal suite at a local hotel.
We were driving North on I-95 traveling from Florida to Maryland. At Emporia, Virginia we pulled into a Holiday Inn. They were filled. I used the corny old standby: "If the President of the United States showed up here tonight, would you have a room for *him*?" The desk clerk was supposed to say, "Of course," then I would cleverly reply, "Well, he's not coming, give us *his* room."

Instead she replied stoically, "We're booked; I would send *him* to our Richmond Holiday Inn."

"How about the bridal suite?" I asked facetiously.

She gave me a big smile and winked, "No problem."

We found chocolates and wedding knickknacks on the circular bed in our room. When we went in to dinner, the waitress grinned and said, "You're the ones in the bridal suite? Here's champagne, compliments of the management."

At first we felt embarrassed as people in the restaurant nodded approvingly and gave us the thumbs-up sign.

Even in the ashes there will be a few sparks.
Russian proverb

The experience was magical. We stopped feeling tired and weary from traveling all day. We giggled, drank champagne, and recalled our wedding and honeymoon. We were paying special attention to each other. It changed a commonplace experience into a romantic interlude. At age seventy, I wasn't twenty-two, but I will *never* forget our night in the Emporia Holiday Inn bridal suite.

Don't ask!

39   Take a weekend mini-vacation.

"Let's drive up to New England and watch the leaves die."

In 1951, while stationed at Fort Benning, Georgia, we planned a weekend mini-vacation in Atlanta. We went with friends, Herb and Sue. Upon arrival at the Peachtree Hotel, we went to our respective rooms. Fran announced she was going to take a bath. I ordered snacks and set-ups from room service.

Fifteen minutes later I was again on the phone, this time talking to Herb—coordinating the evening plans. There was a knock at the door. I yelled, "Come on in."

The room service waiter was an elderly gentleman. He brought in the tray and inquired politely, "Shall I open the club soda bottles, sir?"

Still on the phone, I nodded yes. In those days, in hotels, bottle openers were located in the bathroom—behind the door. Before I had time to open my mouth, the waiter disappeared into the bathroom where Fran was leisurely soaking in the tub.

In a fraction of a second, he was out of the bathroom, and out of the hotel room. Soon Fran appeared—wrapped in a big white bath towel.

"What did you do when he walked in on you?" I asked.

"Oh, it was nothing," she answered calmly. "I put my washcloth in front of my face, so if I ever bumped into him again, he wouldn't recognize me."

40   Give a gift for no reason.

Surprise <u>her</u> with flowers or a book or concert tickets. (They're no surprise on a birthday or anniversary.)

Surprise <u>him</u> with flowers or a six-pack of micro brew or baseball tickets.(A recent study showed that couples who go to ball games together are 23 percent less likely to get divorced.)
Ben White, *The 100 Best Ways to Stay Together*

The scent of the rose will always stay on the hand of the giver.
Chinese proverb

The *best* gift to give your partner is the gift of your attention and understanding to make them feel respected and appreciated. But giving thoughtful gifts—for no reason—is a gracious way of revitalizing your relationship.

"Flowers? That's <u>so</u> arrogant!"

Colored roses have distinctive symbolisms: *Red* signifies love and passion; *Pink* roses express a romantic friendship; *Yellow* denotes friendship and respect; *White* roses represent purity and admiration.

When a man gives a gift "for no reason,"
…there's a reason!

Molly Irving

When I was in the packaging business, we manufactured trivet boxes for Corning Glass. Periodically I would be required to meet in their Steuben Division offices at Fifth Avenue and 56th Street in New York City. On one occasion, I met with their product development manager, David, who had flown down from headquarters in Corning.

After the meeting David was preparing to go to the airport, and I was going to catch the train to Baltimore. He said that when he's in New York, he always stops at Henri Bendel and buys his wife a surprise gift.

If we bestow a gift or favor and expect a return for it, it is not a gift but a trade.

Author unknown

I wanted to appear equally cosmopolitan and said, "I do the very same thing, David."

We cabbed together to the store. He bought perfume, so I bought perfume—then we parted and went our separate ways.

Upon my arrival at home, I gave Fran the expensive perfume and said, "Here's a little surprise for you, darling!"

There was a *lonnnnnng* pause. She looked at me strangely and said, "This is so unlike you. You've never given me gifts when you traveled to New York 'just for the day.' Why, all of a sudden, expensive perfume? And from Henri Bendel's yet!"

"Fran, honey, I am giving you a *gift for no reason.*"

"Bullshit," she replied, "you have a girlfriend, don't you? You're giving me perfume as a bribe because you're feeling guilty. *That's* the only reason. Go fix your own dinner, or better yet, let *her* fix your dinner. My grandmother was right: All men are animals!"

41   Be spontaneous

"Let's get out and do something different today," Fran said.

"It's hot out, and I'm reading a good book," I answered. "Maria invited us to her art show in Fort Pierce, and she said they were having nude models," Fran added.

"Nude models at a public art exhibit, how unusual."

"Well, I think that's what she said."

We drove to Fort Pierce and finally found the right address. It looked more like a rundown trailer park than an art gallery. Two guys blocked the entrance. One was a big fellow with a beard, cap and overalls. The other chap sat on a bicycle wearing an oversized tee-shirt.

"That'll be $6.50 apiece," the man in overalls said.

"Hold on," I answered. "We were invited here to see our friend Maria's artwork."

"Well, if it's your first time at the camp, I'll let you in free. Park, then walk down the trail—you'll hear the music." "Mac," Fran whispered, "that guy on the bike was naked under his tee-shirt!"

"Don't be ridiculous," I replied.

As we approached closer to the music, we saw that everyone was naked. We were in the middle of an art show in a nudist colony. Even the string quartet was naked.

We located Maria (fully dressed) and observed how peaceful, relaxed and calm the scene was. Nudists—of all ages, shapes and sizes—were sunbathing, talking, listening to the music, and viewing Maria's art.

"Stop staring," Fran snapped.

The essence of pleasure is spontaneity.
Germaine Greer

*He who thinks too much
about every step he takes,
will stay on one leg all his life.*
Chinese proverb

"Hey honey, you love to sing," I said. "Why don't you take off your clothes and join the musicians?"

"Are you out of your mind?" she hissed. "I don't care how you do it, get me out of here!"

"You always claim I'm anti-social. The first time I try to be friendly you make a fuss."

As we walked back to the car, we passed a tall, well-endowed, dignified-looking gentleman, ambling down the path towards us—stark naked—talking on his cell phone.

I said to Fran, "Did you see that guy on the cell phone?"

"Cell phone?" she said, "What cell phone?"

42 Plan a party.

For many New Year's Eves, we would take our three sons to Little Italy (in Baltimore), to Maria's Restaurant, until it was no longer *cool* for them to be with their parents on New Year's Eve.

On New Year's Day, we would have an annual open house party, and send unique invitations to our friends, family, business associates, neighbors, and Fran's music and theater colleagues.

1967 party invitation.

The parties were *fun*. Everyone co-mingled in our home. As parents, we can teach children more by our actions and behaviors than by our words. I hope we provided a good example to our sons to accept people for *themselves*, and respect an individual's religious, racial, economic, ethnic background or sexual preference.

Aaron Sopher, our artist friend, sat quietly in a corner sketching. Fran, Ginny, Canter Lipsicus, Ken the oyster shucker, and Henri from Paris entertained with their singing. Sidney, Dr. Bill and the legendary Ray played the piano. Billy was on the conga drums, George on the trap drums, Paula on the flute.

My mother-in-law, Bess, would drink a glass of wine, sit at the piano and hammer out the "head-em off at the pass" music she played in the silent movie theater in Annapolis.

Socialite Sylvia ran out of the bathroom screaming, "My God—a rabbit ran between my legs—no more alcohol!" (Adam was caring for his school rabbit over the Christmas holidays.)

Fran accompanied by
Sidney Raphael.

The well-known psychiatrist, Max, was explaining to my parents why words like "fuck" were perfectly acceptable in the English language. My father wanted to go home.

The star halfback of the Baltimore Colts football team asked Fran to dance. "What kind of work do you do?" she inquired. He wanted to go home, too.

Billy, the bongo player, was describing to a rapt audience of male doctors how the potion he brews in his mixer gives him incredible sexual stamina. The doctors were busy making notes.

George, the artist, drummer and beloved Yoga instructor, told Fran not to come to his Yoga class anymore, because she wouldn't keep quiet or sit still, and it disrupted the group.

Jim had too much to drink and put his car in reverse instead of forward. A tow truck hauled him out of the woods.

Many of the people mentioned are gone. Please don't put off planning parties and doing fun things. A Bulgarian proverb says: *If you want apples, you have to shake the tree.*

Dancers

#43   Travel to interesting places.

Rast ich, so rost ich (When I rest, I rust).
German Proverb

It's important for you and your mate to get away together—just the two of you. Go someplace new and different, whether it's climbing a mountain, walking barefoot on a beach, or driving somewhere impulsively without reservations. Anywhere you can feel *alive.*

On our last big trip, we headed for the city of Vernassa in the Cinque Terre area of Italy. Cinque Terre means *the five territories,* namely the towns of Riomaggiore, Manarol, Corniglia, Vernassa, and Monterosso. Vernassa is a rustic little fishing village on the Ligurian Sea, somewhat isolated, quaint—not bustling with tourists, neon signs, or cars.

To get there we drove south from Genoa to Spezia. I stopped in a small dress shop for directions, and when I said, "Vernassa?" the salesgirl said, "You go choo-choo."

Shaking my head, I rotated my hands, imitating driving a car. Again she persisted, "Non automobile...*Choo-Choo.*"

I persuaded her to draw a map to guide us to Vernassa. There is no direct route. You travel through each of the Cinque Terre cities on a narrow and steep road. It was dusk as we approached the third town, Corniglia. A large fuel truck was coming around the bend in the opposite direction. He stopped and pulled over to the side. I could feel stones sliding into the canyon far below as we narrowly skirted by.

High climbers and deep swimmers never grow old.
German proverb

Fran spoke calmly, "I asked you to stop at Spezia, but no, your macho genetic programming prevented you from listening. Now—thanks to you—we're going to end up dead in a canyon and no one will ever find our bodies!"

When we finally arrived, late at night, on the outskirts of Vernassa, we saw a sign prohibiting non-resident car traffic into town. We carried our luggage and hiked. There were few hotels in Vernassa. We went into a bar to ask for a room. The owner said encouragingly, "Non ci-sono camere." (No rooms) "Andate a La Spezia!" (Go back to Spezia).

After a dinner of fresh linguine in white clam sauce, we asked the young bartender, who spoke English, if there were any rooms. He said, "If you had come in daylight, there were a few available, but at this hour—nothing."

I visualized trekking up the long hill to sleep in our car. Fran approached the man tearfully.

"We've been driving all day. We're exhausted. We're old. Haven't you anything?"

As our host was about to say *no* for the third time, a little old man cooking behind him (his grandfather) started yelling at him in Italian. Suddenly, we had a room. After handing over our passports, we trudged across the square and walked slowly up the five flights to our nest—furnished with small bed, sink, and bidet.

As we fell into bed exhausted, Fran asked, "Where's the bathroom?"

We heard a loud flush right behind our ears, and knew our bed was against the wall of the common toilet. We laughed. When we tried to sleep, we heard the *Choo Choo* noisily stopping at the station, under our window. We

If you don't scale the mountain, you can't view the plain.
Chinese proverb

laughed. When the church bells kept us up by clanging every hour, we laughed.

The next day we explored Vernassa. Cinque Terre is popular with hikers from all over Europe who come to walk the steep and narrow cliff paths overlooking the Ligurian sea, from Monterosso down to Riomaggiore.

I *had* to try hiking. Fran accompanied me up the steep and narrow steps leading from the town to the trail. At the top, out of breath, she said, "I'll wait for you here, please don't be long."

"A man's gotta do what a man's gotta do," I said bravely, "and I gotta hike this trail."

I left Fran and climbed for five minutes to the edge of town, overlooking beautiful Vernassa and the sea far below. As I started north towards Monterosso, the path narrowed and narrowed. I hate heights. I edged forward with my back tight up against the steep cliff wall. "Schmuck," I said to myself, "what are you doing here, you'll get killed."

I turned and crawled back to the wider area, and hiked the few minutes down to where Fran was waiting. I said, "Honey, I hated leaving you alone in a strange place, so I came back."

Fran knowingly said, "That's nice."

Vernassa was an unnerving, uncomfortable, delightful, exciting, and romantic adventure. If you get to Italy, and you want to share some meaningful moments in a small, quaint, seaport town, go to Vernassa. But don't drive, take the *Choo-Choo*.

We do not remember days, we remember moments.
Caesar Pavese

VI Future

Dream your tomorrows, but live your todays

It is a lovely thing to have a husband and wife developing together and having the feeling of falling in love again. That is what marriage really means: helping one another to reach the full status of responsible and autonomous beings who do not run away from life.

Paul Tournier

The best way to make your dreams come true is to wake up.

Paul Valéry

"Yoo-hoo. Time to climb the stairway to paradise."

44 An objective is a dream with a deadline.

As one advances confidently in the direction of his dreams, and endeavors to live the life which he has imagined, he will meet with success unexpected in common hours...and he will live with the license of a higher order of things.
Henry David Thoreau

In *Alice in Wonderland*, Alice said, "If you don't know where you're going, any road will take you there."

It is important to set goals and objectives.

I look to the future, because that's where I'm going to spend the rest of my life.
George Burns

Goals: Goals are dreams and statements of intentions that may be attainable but have *no* deadlines. I am seventy-five years old.

My five-year goals are:

1 Health: To make it to eighty. Then make a new list.

"I'm doing what I can," his doctor explained, "but I can't make you any younger."

"I'm not interested in getting younger," the man told the doctor, "I just don't want to get older."

2 Weight: To lose weight, which will improve my blood pressure and cholesterol, so I can get off medication and see my feet again when I'm showering.

3 Golf: To become a better golfer—and have people invite me to play with them—instead of vice versa.

4 Writing: To become a published writer, so my grandchildren will treat me with respect and my accountant will stop telling me the IRS considers me a hobbyist.

5 Family: To be a better husband, father, and grandfather, because they deserve it.

The beginning is the half of any action.
Greek proverb

Objectives: Objectives are planned and measurable achievements you can verify in a given time frame. My five-year objectives are:

1 Health: To take a brisk thirty-minute walk three times a week, and swim one-quarter mile at least twice a week.

2 Weight: To keep my weight under 185. 180 would be even better. To go to *Weight Watchers* starting next Thursday and "make-it-happen" within ninety days.

3 Golf: To break 90 at golf *this* year. 85 would be even better. To sign up *now* for lessons with Jim, at Arundel Golf Park, and practice at least once per week.

4 Writing: To write five novels over the next five years on subjects that I feel passionate about: namely Haitian Art, Leonardo da Vinci, and three others still incubating.

5 Family: To try and listen more...to listen more...to listen more. And most important: to acknowledge that my wife Fran is *my most important priority!* To keep that thought in mind at times when she's driving me nuts yelling, "Maaac... Maaac...Maaac...can you stop what you're doing and———"

Your objectives: What are the five objectives *you* would most like to accomplish in the next five years? (list them)

1 _____

_____

2 _____

_____

3 _____

_____

To believe a thing is possible is to make it so.
French proverb

4 _____

_____

5 _____

_____

45   Be realistic about sex and money.

"Safe sex is the last thing you need to concern yourself about."

Sex. Sex is *both physical and psychological.* To consider sex as *only* physical is like defining violin music as merely horsehair scraping on catgut. To make sex *only* psychological is to deny mankind's animal origins.

I'm at the age where I think more about food than sex. Last week I put a mirror over our dining room table.
Rodney Dangerfield

Two people met in North Oaks, an assisted-care facility. Both were in their nineties. Since love knows no years, one look was enough for them to know this was it. They were married a week after they met.

On the first night of the honeymoon, they got into bed, held hands and squeezed them.

On the second night, they squeezed hands again.

On the third night, the husband pressed his wife's hand. She said, "Not tonight. I have a headache."

We attended a spa last year, where the psychologist recommended that senior couples, wanting to spice up their physical sexual activity, could purchase *special* educational adult films that were produced by and for seniors.

We bought the films, but Fran felt guilty having tapes of adult erotica lying around the apartment. She thought that if our apartment was robbed, the films would be discovered, and the thieves would lose all respect for her.

Paul Newman's wife, Joanne Woodward, says, "Sexiness wears thin after a while and beauty fades, but to be married to a man who makes you laugh every day, ah, that's a treat."

Money. After retirement, most seniors are on fixed incomes, and therefore budgeting is important. This joint effort will not only give you and your partner a sense of teamwork, but it can reduce the anxiety and arguing that often accompany money matters.

Pleasure may come out of illusion, but happiness can only come out of reality.
Nicholas Chamfort

My wife had her credit card stolen. It's helped us economize. The thief's been spending less than she did.

In our family, Fran manages the expenditures, and she's good at it. I take a monthly amount for discretionary spending. At the last annual budget meeting we had with *God bless Harold*, our accountant, Fran was trying to reduce expenditures. We went over every line item carefully—they were all irreducible. Then we came to *my* discretionary spending amount. Fran had some constructive suggestions.

"You can stop getting haircuts. Long hair is sexy," she suggested. "And if you played golf in the late afternoon, it would be cheaper."

"It gets dark, and I can't finish eighteen holes," I replied. "So what if you only play fourteen holes," Fran added helpfully, "and you should buy your clothes in local thrift shops. They have real bargains."

As a result of our budgetary meeting, I started going around with Fran to the thrift shops. If you could see me in my *almost*-new Ralph Lauren Polo sport jacket, and smashing brown Goodwill Store slacks, you would be impressed.

So what if some guy died in these clothes. Dry cleaning gets out most of the bloodstains.

#46   Cultivate new interests.

> *If you observe a happy man, you will find him building a boat, writing a symphony, growing double dahlias or looking for dinosaur eggs in the Gobi desert. He will have become aware that he is happy in the course of living life twenty-four crowded hours of each day.*
>
> W. Beran Wolfe (1900–1935)

Keep a Green Tree in your heart and perhaps a singing bird will come.
Chinese proverb

Education and exercise are the best ways to prevent cognitive decline, according to a two-and-a-half-year study of 1,200 older people appearing in *Psychology and Aging*.

Consider cultivating new interests like dancing lessons, painting, or buying an RV and caravaning.

Dancing lessons.
While dining in a Chinese restaurant in Jensen Beach, Florida, Fran noticed a group of middle-aged ladies entering the dance studio next door. Curious, she went in and enrolled.

Several weeks later I was typing away, when Fran rushed in breathless. She said, "Don't move."

I heard the stereo turned up. In pranced my wife, wearing black leotards, a black hat, black tap shoes, twirling a baton, and tap-dancing to *New York, New York*. My first shocked reaction was: she might trip on the tile floor and *fracture* something. My second reaction was pure admiration: that Fran, then seventy, would start tap-dancing lessons.

When people asked what I thought about Fran's tap-dancing, I said, "It's fabulous! But we've either got to carpet our entire apartment or increase our insurance."

Enjoy a candlelight dinner.

Some people ask the secret of our long marriage. We take time out to go to a restaurant two times a week. A little candlelight, dinner, soft music and dancing. She goes Tuesdays, I go Fridays.

Henny Youngman

Buy an RV and caravan.

In 1996 David and Dorothy Counts presented a study at the meeting of the American Anthropological Association. They found that retired people who travel around in RV's were healthier, happier and more fundamentally alert than their counterparts in the adult population.

We met Norma on December 3,1999, as she was preparing to leave Fort Pierce, Florida to drive *alone* in her Chevrolet Rainbow Camper van to meet up with some other caravanners in Orlando. From Orlando they were heading to San Benito, Texas. There they were assembling with other members of CARAVAN 2000 to cross the Mexican border at Matamoros and proceed to Veracruz, Mexico, to watch the sun come up over the Gulf of Mexico on "Millennium Morning."

When I asked Norma her age, she gave me a strange look. I changed the subject and asked when she would be returning. "I'll be back around the middle of March," she said, and handed me her card. Under her name, it read:

World Traveler-Gourmet Cook-Picture Taker
Happy Camper-Elderhosteler.

Happiness does not come from happiness itself, but from the journey towards achieving it.

French proverb

#47   Get thee to an Elderhostel.

Elderhostel is a not-for-profit organization with twenty-five years' experience providing affordable, educational adventures for over 175,000 adults per year who are fifty-five and older. These short-term programs are a fun and exciting way for you and your partner to explore new places and make new social contacts.

"Is this the year, Pumpkin? Goodbye, love boat, hello, elder hostel?"

In February 1999 I was in San Diego speaking on the subject of Yellow Pages Advertising at The Moving and Storage Association's annual convention. While there, we stayed an extra week and signed up for an Elderhostel program.

At the first meeting we looked around at all the *old* people.

"Have we made a foolish mistake, coming here?" my wife asked. "This is a far cry from Club Med."

"Maybe it should be called Club Medicare," I added wryly.

After a brief orientation period, the elderly woman on Fran's right introduced herself. "I'm eighty-six years old," she said, "and I'm totally worn out, just traveling here."

Fran patted her arm. "I know, dear, traveling can be exhausting. Where did you come from?"

The nice wrinkled little old lady said, "I just came from rafting down the Colorado River."

That was the beginning of a remarkable week. Not *once* did we hear about aches, pains, operations; or their children who were rich and successful doctors or lawyers; or grandchildren who were talented and beautiful beyond belief. And we didn't hear about how anyone bought Microsoft or GE at just the *right* time.

We heard about *adventures* that people in their sixties, seventies and eighties had experienced in Elderhostel. From physically constructing houses in Appalachia, to art classes in Italy, and canoe trips through the Florida Everglades.

The U.S. Constitution doesn't guarantee happiness, only the pursuit of it. You have to catch up with it yourself.
Benjamin Franklin

*It's never winter
in the land of hope.*
Russian proverb

We had a stimulating and fun week studying Shakespeare, attending the Old Globe Theater, learning about musical comedy and drama, and making new friends. But much more than that, we learned from the example of these remarkable people at Elderhostel, that at any age, life can be enriched by having an open mind, a healthy curiosity, and a willingness to learn and try something new and different.

#48 Ten Commandments for Loving Couples:

Treat yourself to Gregory Godek's book, *1001 Ways to be Romantic*. He calls it a handbook for men and a godsend for women. He advises, "Life is simply too short not to be romantic," and he dedicates the book to *those who want to fall in love again*.

1 Thou shall give 100 percent.
2 Thou shall treat your partner as the unique individual he/she truly is.
3 Thou shall stay connected through word and deed.
4 Thou shall accept change and support growth in yourself and your mate.
5 Thou shall live your love.
6 Thou shall share: The love and fear, the work and play.
7 Thou shall listen, listen, listen.
8 Thou shall honor the subtle wisdom of the heart and listen to the powerful insights of the mind.
9 Thou shall not be a jerk or a nag.
10 Thou shall integrate the *purity* of spiritual love with the *passion* of physical love and the *power* of emotional love.

49   Family matters.

*If one were given five minutes' warning before sudden death,
five minutes to say what it had all meant to us, every telephone
booth would be occupied by people trying to call up other people
to stammer that they loved them.*

Christopher Morley (1890-1957)

*If I am in harmony with
my family, that's success.*
Native American
Ute saying

It's an interesting exercise to contemplate the questions you
would ask, and actions you would take, regarding your
family. Suppose you were suddenly faced with a life
deadline. Consider these questions drawn from the book
How to Think like Leonardo da Vinci, by Michael J. Gelb.

1 How am I perceived by my children and my spouse?

_____

_____

2 What are the blessings of my life?

_____

_____

3 What legacy would I like to leave?

_____

_____

This exercise helps prioritize what is really important. It may encourage you to put aside the hurts and pains every family suffers and to deal with communication, forgiveness and reconciliation.

If I was faced with a life deadline—I would do at least three things: call my sons, contact my grandchildren, and write my wife.

To my three sons, Jamie, Scott and Adam, I would say, "I love you and I'm proud of what you've accomplished and how you are living your lives. In many ways each of you has been *my* role model. Thanks!"

To my grandchildren, Maureen and Harry, I would say, "You will most likely be faced in the not-too-distant future with the opportunity of choosing a life's partner. Choose your spouses carefully. From that one decision may come ninety percent of all your happiness or misery, or maybe both. I would ask you to remember: Be kind to one another.

The greatest wisdom of all is kindness.
Dutch proverb

This is the Golden Rule of marriage and the secret of making love last. Please remember that a successful marriage depends on two things: *Finding the right person...and being the right person.*

Have a great life!"

To my wife, Fran, I would echo her words in a poem she wrote for me entitled "Promises, promises."

50 Keep your promises.

Dearest Fran,

A long time ago you wouldn't promise me
a smile or taste of you with my morning coffee
    Wherever, whenever

You did, however, promise me *rainbows* and lilacs
out of season, and time, time love to grow old with me

You never promised to graft your flesh to mine
and live inside my head
    Whenever, Wherever

You did, however, promise me a song
and time, time love to grow old with me.

Thank you for keeping your promises.

    I love you.

Happy 50th Anniversary

Dear Readers:

Thank you for allowing me to share these thoughts with you. I hope you found a tip or two that will help you travel the sometimes difficult but most meaningful path to a long-lasting relationship.

Fran and I wish you well. Your marriage is important. Please take good care of yourself, be kind to your partner, and try and keep a sense of humor.

Remember if you want the rainbow, you gotta put up with the rain. That's just how it is.

Best of luck,
Mac Mahr

Index of Sources

Foreward
Dolly Parton
Erica Jong
Fran Mahr, "Promises, Promises" (1974).

CHAPTER 1
Ben White, *The 100 Best Ways to Stay Together.*
Dell Pub Co. (March 1998).
Carl Sandburg

CHAPTER 4
Nikki Giovanni, *Cotton Candy on a Rainy Day* (1979).
Liv Ullman
Doyle Barnett, *20 Communication Tips for Couples,*
New World Library (Sept. 1995).
Phyllis McGinley
Thomas Chandler

CHAPTER 5
Submitted excerpt from *Men Are from Mars, Women Are from Venus* by John Gray. Copyright (c) 1992 by John Gray.
Reprinted by permission of Harper Collins Publishers Inc.

CHAPTER 6
Clifford Notarius & Howard Markman, *We Can Work It Out,*
Perigee Reprint edition (November 1994).

CHAPTER 7
Michael Nichols, *The Lost Art of Listening,* Guilford Press (1995).
Paul Tillich
Stephen Covey

CHAPTER 9
Sri Sarada Deci
Michael P. Nichols, *The Lost Art of Listening,*
Franklin P. Jones

CHAPTER 10
William Shakespeare, *Hamlet*, Act 1, Sc.3.
Ralph Waldo Emerson

SECTION III
Fran Mahr

CHAPTER 11
Jimmy Carter. From *Always a Reckoning and Other Poems* by
Jimmy Carter, copyright © 1955 by Jimmy Carter. Used by
permission of Times Books, a division of Random House.
Doyle Barnett, *20 Communication Tips for Couples,* New
World Library (Sept. 1995).

CHAPTER 12
John Gottman. From *The Seven Principals for Making Marriage Work*
by John M. Gottman, Ph.D. and Nan Silver, copyright © 1999
by John M. Gottman, Ph. D. and Nan Silver. Used by
permission of Crown Publishers, a division of Random
House, Inc.
Chris Rock

CHAPTER 13
John Gottman, *The Seven Principals for Making Marriage Work.*

CHAPTER 15
Michael P. Nichols, *The Lost Art of Listening.*
Jackie Carter
Risa Mickenberg, *Taxi Driver Wisdom,* Chronicle Books (June 1996).

CHAPTER 16
Phyllis Diller
Milton Berle

CHAPTER 17
Thomas Jefferson, *A Decalogue of Canons for Observation in
Practical Life* (1825).
Charles Spieberger, Ph.D.
Dr. Joyce Brothers
Aristotle

CHAPTER 28
Samuel Johnson
George Burns
James Michener

CHAPTER 29
Howard Rankin, *10 Steps to a Great Relationship,* Stepwise Pr. (April 1998).

CHAPTER 30
Kahlil Gibran. From *The Prophet* by Kahlil Gibran, copyright 1923 by Kahlil Gibran and renewed 1951 by Administrators C.T.A. of Kahlil Gibran Estate and Mary G. Gibran. Used by permission of Alfred A. Knopf, a division of Random House, Inc.
Ranier Maria Rilke

CHAPTER 31
Mitch Albom, *Tuesdays with Morrie,* Broadway Books (Oct. 2002).

CHAPTER 32
Carl Sandburg. "Happiness" from *Chicago Poems* by Carl Sandburg, copyright 1916 by Holt, Rinehart and Winston and renewed 1944 by Carl Sandburg, reprinted by permission of Harcourt, Inc.
Fran Mahr, "Surfer Man."
Muriel Dobbin, *Baltimore Sun* (May 1964).
Jonas Salk
Frank A. Clark

CHAPTER 33
Bess Schleider

CHAPTER 34
Marriage Partnership magazine (Oct. 1999)
Robert S. Elliot

CHAPTER 35
Zen Master Dogen
Max Kaufman

CHAPTER 48

Gregory Godek. Copyright © 1995 by Gregory Godek. Reprinted from the book *1001 Ways to be Romantic* with the permission of its publisher Sourcebooks, Inc. (800-432-7444).

CHAPTER 49

Christopher Morley
Michael J. Gelb, *How to Think Like Leonardo da Vinci,* Dell (Feb. 2000).

CHAPTER 50

Madame DeSevigne